Bertrand Tavernier

Fractured Narrative and Bourgeois Values

Emily Zants

The Scarecrow Press, Inc.
Lanham, Maryland, and London
1999

SCARECROW PRESS, INC.

Published in the United States of America
by Scarecrow Press, Inc.
4720 Boston Way
Lanham, Maryland 20706

4 Pleydell Gardens, Folkestone
Kent CT20 2DN, England

British Library Cataloguing in Publication Information Available

Library of Congress Cataloging-in-Publication Data
Zants, Emily.
    Bertrand Tavernier : fractured narrative and bourgeois values /
Emily Zants.
      p. cm.
    Filmography: p.
    Includes bibliographical references and index.
    ISBN 0-8108-3627-0 (cloth : alk. paper)
    1. Tavernier, Bertrand—Criticism and interpretation. I. Title.
PN1998.3.T377Z66 1999
791.43'0233'092—dc21   98-53128
                                        CIP

♾™ The paper used in this publication meets the minimum requirements of
American National Standard for Information Sciences—Permanence of
Paper for Printed Library Materials, ANSI Z39.48–1984.
Manufactured in the United States of America.

Dedicated to my nephew's son,
Kyle David Hartman

Contents

Illustrations

Preface

Bertrand Tavernier's style is nonhierarchical, a style that has a long and established history in European films, but one that is not sanctioned by Hollywood. Since impressionism, European art has stressed the nonhierarchical, nonlinear approach as a means of engaging the spectator in the new vision the artist wishes to communicate. Recent scientific explorations, often called Chaos Theory or Complexity, have indicated that the patterns in events are more significant than the causal sequences, something known by artists for over a century. So the nonlinear approach would appear to be the way of the future, whether in European or American films.

An art form that is serious always attempts to enlarge our vision of reality or see it from a new perspective. This kind of art requires participative viewing, a form of enjoyment that is becoming more and more foreign to Americans. Hollywood has taught Americans to consider film as an escape, as spectacle, to go for entertainment, not solutions to problems. As a consequence, Americans quite often misunderstand European films because they expect the entertainment that was never intended to be there. French films generally try to involve the spectators, prompting them to bring their personal experiences to the film. They require an active form of viewing, something for which many Americans have no habit; they only know how to watch a film in the passive mode. And a number of American film critics have fallen into the same frame of mind.

Another tenet of the Hollywood spectacle demands that the "good guy" wins. All forms of violence are acceptable entertainment on that one condition. Films that show battles where the powerful self-destruct, as in Patrice Chéreau's marvelous *Queen Margot,* are usually condemned as gratuitously brutal and violent. Few are understood to illustrate the self-destructive nature of ultimate power. Though

Americans understand rationally and intellectually that the use of the hydrogen bomb probably means self-destruction by making the air and water unusable, no American-born individual has a living memory of another power physically invading the homeland. Almost all Europeans have some living family member who has experienced just that phenomenon. To the European, there is nothing salutary about power. Military force can conquer nations, but when taken too far, it provokes revolts that will bring about its demise.

The United States did not dare use the H-bomb to win in Vietnam, for no country in the world would have trusted us thereafter. International commerce would have dwindled tremendously and Americans would not have been able to travel to foreign countries without suffering recriminations. Instead of having allies, the rest of the world would have allied against us. Knowing this, we still relegate power of that scope to war alone. Somehow it's not supposed to be related to business practices.

When individuals speak against the hierarchical power structure, Americans generally assume their motivation must be communism or socialism, perhaps because the nations that we know oppose our system of free enterprise have been communist or socialist nations. The most successful businesses in the United States today, however, have been practicing cooperation, or a mutual sharing of input, instead of the more traditional top-down management that led to Big Blue's crash in the 1980s. To regain its place on Wall Street, IBM called in management consultants and had to learn Microsoft's business approach. Bill Gates is the world's richest man because he listens to the best input he can get, regardless of paycheck. No one considers Microsoft to be a communist or even a socialist enterprise! Many other companies have discovered that top-down management was leading them to bankruptcy; they are still cutting back on top-level bosses. They discovered that employee shareholding was more productive than ownership by outside investors. Adopting employee ownership certainly didn't make airline companies in the United States socialist or communist ventures.

The most striking model, perhaps, for the nonhierarchical structure is the Internet. No site controls another. Though one page may branch to others, even the most distant branch can be directly accessible without passing through a specific hierarchy of other branches first. This lateral structure has proven to be more competitive than either the hierarchical or the socialist structure. It is participative as well as collaborative. Significantly, no linear plot development controls it. Congress is confounded by this nonhierarchical structure it cannot control.

Though Bertrand Tavernier is a communist, he never uses film for propaganda. His manner of exposing the power structure and the prejudices that perpetuate its injustices is equally relevant to European and American endeavors. Tavernier is fond of quoting Michelet's statement: "To deal with history, you have to unlearn respect." This study is offered to further an understanding of both Bertrand Tavernier's work and his techniques for breaching the frozen forms of thought generated by centuries of hierarchical thinking.

1

Introduction

Bertrand Tavernier has been called France's leading director by Martin Scorcese (Hoffman 1985, 96), and *pour cause*. He is one of those rare masters who can change our prejudices between the beginning and end of a film. Rimbaud wrote poetry "to change the world." Tavernier has never been so pretentious. He just changes spectators one after another. He unsettles them because he undermines the hierarchical power structure, violating the causal narrative conventions that support it.

The world cannot evolve with all our old prejudices in place. The problem with most would-be revolutionaries is that they try to tell us exactly what our new prejudices should be. It would be comforting to know ahead of time what we can believe in after letting go of old prejudices. But Tavernier never comforts the viewer by providing new solutions. He merely unsettles the old habits, abandoning the viewer on the sidewalk, alone, to seek new solutions that do not perpetuate old problems.

Truly new solutions cannot be found until the frozen forms of thought that generated the problems have been dispelled. Tavernier's main enterprise is freedom from old preconceptions to allow for the birth of new ideas and new relationships. These new relationships cannot be predicted ahead of time. They can only materialize as a body of participants forms that is capable of adapting to and living by new ideas. First must come freedom from bondage to old forms of thought.

Tavernier achieves this transformation of the viewers by using techniques explored by writers such as Proust and Joyce, but incorporating them into the now century-old cinematic vocabulary. Essentially, the fundamental techniques involve the destruction of narrative. In film, this could easily be found in Buñuel's or Resnais's films. But whereas Buñuel remained outrageous and Resnais intellectual, Tavernier destroys narrative by serving the spectator an all too familiar world, then fracturing the apparently seamless structure by violating the anticipated form, the cause and effect development that is part and parcel of the linear hierarchical system. For this reason, you enter Tavernier's films feeling safe and secure, but you do not leave feeling the same way.

Usually misunderstood by critics he receives little of the fanfare in the United States that European critics give avant-garde directors, especially if part of a new school or artistic movement with its own manifesto. His profound originality has received little attention for at least two reasons: his films are deceptively realistic and he does not proclaim a specific doctrine. Still, his films inevitably carry his stamp. Exploring this uniqueness is the intent of this work.

Artists appear to have a new vision of the world because we are blinded by the older, familiar ways of perceiving our surroundings, communicated to us by our culture. Every culture has boundaries, basic beliefs that help preserve it as a culture. But some of these beliefs often prevent evolution. And a culture that cannot evolve will eventually die. Consonant with modern scientific theories stressing the inter-relationships between events as more important than their sequential order (Chaos Theory, Complexity), Tavernier always seeks to reveal an aspect of those relationships that has been obscured by socio-political conformity.

Many of his characters have difficulty communicating because of this conformity. As a result they suffer from the exclusion. Communication occurs within a system only when the ideas and feelings expressed are familiar, *déjà vu*. Individuals experience crises within any given system when they have new concepts and relationships to express, but there is no framework to accommodate them. These are the truly creative individuals who are showing paths for evolution. Some are broken by the system. Most are recognized for their foresight only after their death or when they are too old or sick to care. Many of Tavernier's characters are creative people: the Regent in *Let Joy Reign Supreme*, the teacher Nathalie Baye in *A Week's Vacation*, the reporter Harvey Keitel and the writer Romy Schneider in *Death Watch*, the writer Michel Piccoli in *Spoiled Children*, the daughter Irene in *A Sunday in the Country*, the saxaphonist in *'Round Midnight* and the writer-daughter of *Daddy Nostalgia*. The challenge consists in breaching the frozen forms of a culture so that new relationships can be perceived and fostered. Tavernier is master at breaching the walls of Western culture, particularly those of the hierarchical power structure.

Numerous prejudices are inherent in that structure. To attack the prejudices directly would reduce his films to mere political polemics. The more a system is attacked directly, the stronger the defense of its frozen forms. Tavernier's films rarely descend to that level, and only momentarily, for he "detests doctrines" because they prevent people from recognizing the problem, restricting the possibilities for answers. His films attack prejudices by ripping them open, exposing bleeding hearts, plunging the spectators into the entrails of the hierarchical power structure and leaving them there to extract themselves as best they can. He does not provide conclusions. Rather he opens the playing field to allow better solutions to contemporary problems. The spectators are introduced to parts of themselves they had not met before, a part pushed into the subconscience by social models of conformity. Tavernier's great talent is his success in revealing the spectators' prejudices to themselves, making them embarrassed to repeat the clichés acceptable to society so that its closed form can be sustained and perpetuated. More than any other filmmaker, perhaps, Tavernier disrupts bourgeois comfort. His ability not only to involve the spectators in initial acceptance of a given prejudice but to alter their commitment to that position by the end of the film constitutes the essence of his uniqueness and originality. In *Clean Slate*, for instance, the police chief first appears to us as a pitiful excuse for a man; by the end of the film we do not know whether to fear him, respect him, or pray he is our best friend.

The way he achieves this transformation is to dismantle plot or causal story development as the basis of film. His protagonist is never a hero, but John Doe Everyman. There are no big events. Take plot, heroes, and spectacular events away from a Hollywood film and nothing is left. Tavernier does that and ends up with a profoundly moving film. How? And in what way does plot destruction coincide with breaches in the walls of the hierarchical power structure?

To start with the latter of these questions will launch us into a full exploration of Tavernier's art, the purpose of this book. Suffice it to suggest at this point that causal plot development is essential to power structures and helps sustain belief in them. A hero, or power symbol, is accorded that stature precisely because he (or she) has performed certain acts that warrant that recognition. The relationship is causal. Characteristically in France, acquisition of heroic stature not only permits, but almost demands, that you reign over others, like General de Gaulle, for example. American heroes, on the contrary, ride on to help the next person in need, especially in westerns. That distinction between the two nationalities warrants a book in itself, and Tavernier would no longer be the principal subject matter. The hypothesis is relevant here because it suggests to some extent Tavernier's incredible attraction for much that is American, especially jazz and Hollywood B-movies, while execrating the importance accorded the individual in American culture. Indeed, a look at this appeal of jazz and B-movies is essential to a comprehension of Tavernier's revelatory techniques.

But first, who is Bertrand Tavernier?

Biographical Background

Tavernier was born into a literary family in Lyons in 1941: his father was already a writer. Bertrand was supposed to be studying for the law exams but the Cinémathèque Française was located next door. When he turned in a blank sheet of paper for his exams, his parents said he would have to start paying rent. In the early 1960s he wrote extensively for film magazines, especially *Positif* and *Cahiers du cinéma*, but he became disenchanted with their attacks on filmmakers and founded a film club devoted to showing B-movies (Yakir 1984, 18).

Impressed with *Bob le Flambeur*, he obtained an interview with the director Jean-Pierre Melville, working with him in 1961 as trainee for assistant production manager. The effect was enriching, but in a negative sense: he found Melville's cold and dictatorial method of directing deadening on the actors and promised himself he would never provoke that stifling an atmosphere on a set. By all accounts, he has succeeded remarkably in creating both a relaxed and creative atmosphere, allowing all to contribute. Because of Melville, who limited himself to detective films, Tavernier also determined to try different genres. He found that all of Melville's films began to resemble one another, limiting Melville (Bonneville 1982, 25-28). He has diversified so successfully that critics cannot pigeonhole him. He therefore remains an enigma to most. Tavernier began working as a press agent in 1962, quitting only in 1972 to make *The Clockmaker*, and since then has enjoyed solid and regular commercial success.

During that same period, he collaborated with various film periodicals as a film critic and produced his first short films.

In 1962 he married the Irish scriptwriter Claudine (Colo) O'Hagan who soon bore him a daughter, Tiffany, and then a son, Nils. After fifteen years together, they separated but have often collaborated on film scripts since (Coulombe and Wera 1988, 15). In 1977 Tavernier founded his own production company, Little Bear.

Though he has built up his own cinematic family, working best with a team that he knows well, members of the team change from time to time because Tavernier fears the deadening effect of routine and is excited by the new directions in which new team members can take him. Philippe Noiret has been the lead actor in many of his films, and has become his best friend. Pierre-William Glenn, director of photography, and others have become just as familiar on the set, however different the film may be. Glenn noted that working with Tavernier was a unique experience because "he leaves people a lot of liberty which makes them trust him and want to bring him something as well. He completely validates the idea of cinema as a collective work where each person is a driving force" (Bion 1984, 86). In his movies, everyone contributes something creative to the final work. He remains the *auteur* because he knows not only how to accept the ideas of others, but to give them value in the work as a whole, as did Jean Renoir.

Any attempt to categorize Tavernier's films by subject matter or genre is futile. The opening voice-over of *A Sunday in the Country* could well be his *devise*: "When will you stop asking even more from life, Irene?" The question is that of Irene's now defunct mother and Irene's hyper-activity seems to reflect that of Tavernier himself, who, making films and writing their scripts, is president of the Société des Réalisateurs de Films as well as L'Institut Lumière in Lyons while co-authoring the best encyclopedia of American film to date. A brilliant and curious individual, he is fascinated by almost any social, political or human problem that results from taboos. Such themes include the fear of conformism and dehumanization, the impulse towards protest and revolt, the difficulties of effectively realizing such a protest in action, and the questioning of authority and power. The resultant and more intimate problems of isolation and lack of communication are equally present. All of Tavernier's films are films of love, of passion, of intense emotional experiences. They all deal with the extraordinary difficulty a human being has communicating the most profoundly felt emotions to others. Such communication seems to occur only under exceptional circumstances that permit the individual to escape isolation, if only for a brief time.

Tavernier is particularly fond of historical periods that are *in transit*. The old values no longer appear valid; the principles of order, the frozen forms of the establishment have been questioned. Answers, however, are neither clearly spelled out nor readily available (Bertin-Maghit 1980, 109; B.B. and D.R.-B. 1992, 59). The use of transitional periods of history appeals to Tavernier for many reasons. First, they contain similarities to our own period of transition. Second, they are not as wellknown since they are not the moments of a society's crowning glory; their interpretations are not already cast in bronze. Therefore, they cater to disrespectful attitudes that put the conventions behind them in question, that can lead us to a better understanding of history and in potentially new directions.

By exploring different themes and emotions, Tavernier is exploring his own possibilities of self-realization. This tendency even explains the unique partnership that has developed between him, as director, and Philippe Noiret, an actor he has cast in extremely diverse roles, almost all of which he claims are the expression of something felt within himself. When asked about his very diverse cinematic interests, he said: "The only thing I try to do is to set up a completely different challenge for myself with each new film, to use what I learned from previous films to put myself in question again and never have the least feeling of comfort" (Cèbe 1981, 27). Of *Clean Slate* he said,

> I made the film because I was angry at the time. . . . I wanted to break the image of my nobility, because I was being labeled as a humanist director, and I wanted to show a kind of dark, violent side, which I have and which I think I present in all my films. . . . it shows the fear I have in me. . . . Making such a film in a way is a kind of joke, but it's real, too, it's a way of curing yourself of some hate you have, or some fear or some anger. It prevents you from killing a few people. (Hurley 1983, 232-33)

Noiret, who also dislikes being categorized, has said,

> what I like about being a leading actor is to wait and see what the director thinks of me and what he feels I can do. Sometimes, I am very surprised. When Bertrand gave me some of these recent parts, I was shocked. I would never think of casting myself in some of these roles, never. (Hurley 1982, 164)

American Influences

More than anyone perhaps, Tavernier is responsible for recognition of the contribution to film provided by B-movies, the western in particular. And he is addicted to jazz, having made, to date, what is considered the best film dealing with it. Understanding the appeal of these elements elucidates some of the characteristics of his own films.

Jazz

The improvisational nature of jazz appeals to Tavernier: "I strive for a loose, musical structure" (Coursodon 1986, 23). In his own films he incorporates seemingly extraneous material that surfaces during production into the film itself, enriching its texture. He is always exploring; a script does not set the action in concrete. If something happens during a shoot, Tavernier is likely to incorporate it, such as events or statements made by actors on the set that were not scripted. In his jazz film *'Round Midnight*, when the musician Dale, played by Dexter Gordon, has just agreed to return to Paris with his best friend Francis (but does not), Dale says: "You know, Francis, there is not enough kindness in the world." Dexter had heard another musician quote this from *The Mask of Dimitrios*[1] several weeks earlier; he said it unexpectedly during rehearsal and Tavernier kept it as the last words we hear from Dale. It reads like his epitaph (Coursodon 1986, 18-19). Tavernier had asked another musician "why Dexter at times seemed bent on destroying himself, and he answered, 'Maybe he's afraid he no longer has anything to give'" (Coursodon 1986, 22). Tavernier kept it as a remark by Dale-Dexter.

From master scriptwriter Jean Aurenche, Tavernier learned the freedom of incorporating all of life into a film. If he hears a phrase he likes while filming, it will most likely be incorporated into the film. The result is most engaging: the spectator is prompted to find an explanation—just as he does for coincidental things in life. But the technique also makes a richer, more dense film. When he was filming *'Round Midnight*, one of the jazz musicians, Wayne Shorter, paid him what Tavernier considered to be the biggest compliment, "you are doing this film exactly as we make our music, by listening all the time the same way we are listening to the notes, taking, grabbing something, taking it, using it" (Jacobowitz et al. 1986, 70).

Critics stuck on a strict adherence to a sequential storyline inevitably take offense at these additions and may have little appreciation for the improvisational nature of jazz as well. Extraneous, improvised events or scenes help fragment an apparently realistic, recognizable bourgeois setting. As Dale explains to Francis, "I heard Lester Young and he was playing all those color tones, 6ths and 9ths and major 7ths like Debussy." Tavernier's apparent asides are like the color tones of jazz. The viewer sees a familiar world and then the logic is not exactly what was anticipated; a new color was added.

Jazz represents the spontaneity, the freedom and potential of another form of thought not yet determined. In post-World War II France, jazz brought a breath of fresh air. Though the expression of an oppressed culture, it seemed free of the European forms of thought that had brought about that war. As in jazz, Tavernier's scenarios focus on the crosscurrents of the present, with little exposition or attempt to justify the present by the past. In 'Round Midnight, for instance, we know instinctively the lovely singer Darcy Lee must be an old flame of Dale's, but all we are shown is their happiness of the moment as she belts out "How Long Has This Been Going On?" The song could apply to their personal experience or any of the themes of the movie. One of Tavernier's reasons for selecting bebop jazz was because it was "outside the system. . . . [B]ebop is the only part of the American music which has never been recuperated, swallowed, by the system. I mean, Broadway has used the blues, has used Fats Waller, Duke Ellington. They took everything" (Dempsey 1987, 5). This absorption, or reduction of all that is new to fit into established structures is abhorrent to Tavernier.

'Round Midnight (1986)

The film was born when Martin Scorcese, the mutual friend of Tavernier and Irwin Winkler (producer for Scorcese's New York, New York and Raging Bull) introduced them at lunch where they discovered their love of jazz. Winkler was interested because "Other than film, jazz is one of the true cultural phenomena given to the world. The tragedy is that film has almost completely ignored jazz" (Hoffman 1985, 110). A photograph of Lester Young in Paris had captured Tavernier's imagination and was the "root of [his] desire to make such a film" (Coursodon 1986, 20). As his co-scriptwriter, he chose David

Rayfiel with whom he had worked six years earlier for *Deathwatch*. A musician told him that if he wanted to develop relationships he "needed a non-musician character to play opposite [the] protagonist." Tavernier found the bare storyline in the true relationship between pianist Bud Powell and Francis Paudras, an amateur pianist in love with the jazz he heard in Paris at such clubs as The Blue Note. Paudras told Tavernier that he would crouch outside the club to listen to Powell's music through a vent. "He spoke of checking Bud in and out of hospitals, taking care of him, getting him ready for his return to New York, a 'comeback' that actually was to kill him" (Coursodon 1986, 20). Once given the source of the plot, critics immediately chose to dwell on the changes Tavernier made to real facts in the life of Bud Powell, though there had never been the pretense of a documentary. Tavernier did a jazz documentary: *Mississippi Blues* would be the film to criticize if infidelity to fact were the question, but there is little criticism of that film for its infidelity. There critics complain that reality does not have a better storyline!

Mississippi Blues documents an era in jazz as well as African-American history. That two Whites, his partner Robert Parish, and himself obtained permission to take cameras and crew inside Negro churches, bars, and homes to record the extraordinary Blues and spiritual performances that were still part of the living South is a feat in itself. They are extraordinarily privileged performances. The film stands as a testimony to the neglect and oversight American culture has evidenced to the contribution of jazz to the world.

In the 1960s, when I was doing graduate studies at Columbia University, Ella Fitzgerald was scheduled to perform, once again, at the famous New York theater where she made her debut: the Apollo theater in Harlem, just "below" Columbia and Morningside Heights. I had two male friends reared in New York, one Jewish and one Catholic, who consented to escort me to the performance. We went early the night of the performance to stand in line for tickets. No other Whites were present. Upon entering we immediately proceeded to the back row of the balcony to remain as inconspicuous as possible. And when everyone rose to cry Hallelujah, we stood too; when the audience clapped, we clapped. It was my first experience of "sitting at the back of the bus." Soon after that, Harlem was closed to Whites. I still feel amazingly lucky to have been allowed to participate in one of Ella Fitzgerald's last performances (perhaps the last) at the Apollo theater. This same extraordinarily privileged view of a music, a culture, and an epoch in American history is what Tavernier provides in *Mississippi Blues*. Between this documentary and *'Round Midnight*, he has provided us with two treasures of our own culture—with or without a storyline.

Films

B-movies so intrigued Tavernier that, long before he even became a film critic, he founded a film club, the Nickelodéon, where he showed the films of such directors as Bud Boetticher, Samuel Fuller, Gordon Douglas, Douglas Sirk, King Vidor, and Delmer Daves, directors ignored by the New Wave movement and the *Cahiers* critics of the 1960s. Tavernier's *50 ans de cinéma américain* (co-authored with Jean-Pierre Coursodon, 1991) has been deemed a more comprehensive dictionary of American film than anything written in English. The 1991 edition is an extensively updated version of their 1963 *30 ans de cinéma américain;* in the latest edition they add revised opinions of earlier entries as well as more information. From these directors and others—Tavernier has favorite directors in all nationalities—he garnered a whole arsenal of cinematic approaches and freely moves among them depending on the subject at hand. The intent of looking at major characteristics of B-movies that attracted Tavernier is to glimpse at the main source of some of his own esthetic concepts, and in no way wishes to exclude influences numerous others have had on him.

(1) Understanding of the ignored or outcast rather than the hero. In many American filmmakers he found a voice given to the oppressed and a sympathy and understanding accorded them, as in John Ford's *Grapes of Wrath*. The underdog or historically vanquished individual becomes interesting to us because Tavernier categorically disregards the politically correct version of history, letting the oppressed such as the rapist Bouvier in *The Judge and the Assassin* speak for himself, developing sympathy for the assassin and exposing the prejudices of the judge for what they are: prejudices, not justice. The judge proclaims the absolute need of society to banish vagabonds as detrimental to its values. But the butcher-rapist Bouvier reveals himself as the consequences of those values. He was commended for killing in war, a war defending his country and its values. But society had no place for a man with those talents once the war was over. Raped by priests while at the seminary, he cannot even get the Church to permit him to sweep floors. Suddenly the judge's would-be righteous values no longer

appear so just. The dissolute Bouvier becomes more interesting than the judge, exposing many of society's values as semi-clichés. Still he is criminal by accident, a banal offspring of society's injustices, not a criminal in the heroic nature of a Mafia gang leader.

All of Tavernier's historical works deal with the vanquished, not the victors of history books. In *The Clockmaker* the youth in revolt are shown as the oppressed, not derelict delinquents. They revolt because they are ignored by society as was Bouvier, or a farmer in *The Grapes of Wrath*. Almost every adult but the father wants to interpret the murder by the son as a crime of passion because the private factory guard who was murdered had harassed his girlfriend. No adult wants to hear his political reason: the *salauds* always win over others. The youth who work hard do not have a chance. They revolt because they are oppressed, not because they are delinquent.

(2) Part good, part bad. Delmer Daves's film *Broken Arrow* (starring Jimmy Stewart making peace between the Apaches and the Whites) tackled the problem of racism in the guise of the western where Daves refused to see things in black and white terms, where some Whites are as blood-thirsty as Apaches and some Apaches as honorable as some Whites. Similarly none of Tavernier's characters is all good or all bad. Often the spectators think a character is a loser in the beginning and discover he was at least human and had some touching qualities before the end. All his films are examples of this characteristic, which will be explored in depth as part of his realism.

(3) Characters integrated into the social fabric and set. Another trait he discovered in B-films, which he already admired in Balzac and Zola, was the projection of the society that produced the oppressed, "When I interviewed some of these directors later, I found out that this was very deliberate on their part. This is another way the American cinema strongly influenced me" (Coursodon 1986, 23). The social context is implicit in the sets, the environment of the individuals. The psychological or moral solitude of the B-film protagonist—often a hero by virtue of this solitude—is preempted by the isolation of his physical surroundings, an easy correspondence to establish in a western. In the same manner, the lonely police chief of *Clean Slate* is relegated to the obscure little town of Bourkassa, lost somewhere in Africa.

Tavernier particularly values films in which the setting allows the complexity of an emotion to be better understood, not where it is used to merely sell an emotion (Tavernier 1981, 73). Emotions being the heart of Tavernier cinema, what he admired in King Vidor was "his cosmic apprehension of the world, of relationships between the Individual, Nature, Creation," as well as "the excess of feelings." The harmony of individual acts with the setting is paramount for Tavernier, and thus he admires Vidor because he can do "an extremely provocative love scene where the protagonists are one with the elements surrounding them" (Coursodon and Tavernier 1991, 956). Similarly, of Samuel Fuller he writes,

> What is beautiful about Fuller's productions is that they end up making things "organic" that, taken separately, are hardly realistic. In Fuller, the setting becomes integrated with the principal characters, who no longer notice the violence around them, for they perform it automatically with no notion of a personal act. (Lajeunesse et al. 1981, 82-83)

He likes John Ford because his heroes always need help (Liberty Valence), that is, need a social milieu to support them. The New Wave's admiration of Howard Hawks, however, met with reserve in Tavernier because he found Hawks too devoted to the individual without a sense of the social context. For Tavernier, the filmmaker himself brings with him the sense of his own place or setting. Just as King Vidor remained a Texan in his search for higher truths, so Tavernier seeks to remain French. Thus, he transposed the American book's setting for *Clean Slate* to a provincial French African town.

(4) Questioning the status quo. Tavernier could write of himself what he said of Samuel Fuller, "there is a will to upset archetypes, a desire to take the opposite stand of everything that surrounds him" (Lajeunesse et al. 1981, 81). As in Tavernier's best films, "Ford is also attracted to periods that are distressed, to the moment when one world disappears to make way for a new society, often at the cost of heavy sacrifices (John Wayne in *The Searchers* or *Liberty Valence*)" (Coursodon and Tavernier 1991, 480). Tavernier has a categorical bias against the *parti pris* of Hollywood in favor of the individual over the group and Nature over Civilization (Coursodon and Tavernier 1991, 481). His introduction to the extensive Robert Altman entry in his *Cinquante ans de cinéma américain* could also stand as his own, "Altman's entire career is placed under the sign of provocative iconoclasm, defiance; . . . he bends over backwards to upset the comfort of the spectator" (Coursodon and Tavernier 1991, 274-75). His own realism will do just that.

(5) Destruction of storyline. One of the ways he found that Altman questioned the spectators' comfort was by "dynamiting" the concept of a storyline, "multiplying points of view and levels of narration . . . the destruction of linearity" (Coursodon and Tavernier 1991, 275). What he liked in both John Ford and Howard Hawks was their tendency to destroy plot. In *The Big Sleep*, "you don't have any plot. . . . you discover that once you have characters the plot doesn't count" (Kemp 1994, 18).

All of these characteristics lead us to the enigma of Tavernier's art: his realism is ruptured by improvisations, by violations to the traditional causal storyline with its beginning, middle, and end. Upon examination, his realism turns out to be disruptive after seducing the spectators into an apparently familiar world. His disrespect for the principles of storytelling, for heroes, and great events, undermines the spectators' anticipations of success within the hierarchical structure. The structure itself becomes uncomfortable by the end of a Tavernier film.

Notes

1. A 1944 Peter Lorre and Sydney Greenstreet movie adapted from Eric Ambler's novel *A Coffin for Dimitrios*.

2

Realism in Transition

Tavernier's films are firmly grounded in French roots, but he uses this particular reference to reveal more universal principles. France is a microcosm of the general laws that apply overall. This realistic facade often conceals his profound originality, yet it is essential to engaging the spectators in the filmic experience. Robin Wood notes,

> Realism has frequently been a cover for the reproduction and reinforcement of dominant ideological assumptions, and to this extent that attack is salutary. Yet Tavernier's cinema demonstrates effectively that the blanket rejection of realism rests on very unstable foundations. Realism has been seen as the bourgeoisie's way of talking to itself. It does not necessarily follow that its only motive for talking to itself is the desire for reassurance. (1990, 833)

Tavernier's films are not reassuring and thereby demonstrate that helpless passivity is not the only position allowed the spectator of realist fiction. His films demand the viewer's involvement. This is generally obtained by placing the viewer squarely in front of the social niceties that cover up a problem and revealing them as nothing but superficial conventions. In *Clean Slate*, for example, he rips apart the myth that the strongest character is the one who publicly demonstrates control over others. The pimps who push the police chief around in front of his own servants are later secretly executed by the police chief. Still, the local society thinks the pimps are stronger.

His interest in history is not that of the 1950s *cinéma de qualité,* which looked to great historical events and heroes for depth, a tendency the New Wave deplored. Tavernier is interested in the "new history"

currents which forego political events and look to the everyday social
and economic causes and consequences as more revealing of problems.
Because of his return to history, however, many critics initially
assumed he was a traditional realist, which he is not, for he uses
uncelebrated historical events to find a different point of view.

Characters in Context

His protagonists are frequently bourgeois: "troubled, questioning,
caught up in social institutions but not necessarily rendered impotent by
them, capable of growth and awareness" (Wood 1990, 834). As
Tavernier himself noted, "It's my obsession to be interested in people
who work, who scramble, who are confronted by the earth. . . . And
it's also the opposite of the American ideology which privileges the
individual cut off from the group and only developing fully when
alone" (Tavernier 1990, 55-56). Unless the traditional shot/countershot
can be done asymmetrically, he avoids it because it isolates individuals,
in effect separates them. His characters always function within a group
that provides a social context.

Above all, his characters are integrated into a cultural and physical
milieu. Tavernier has a strong sense of cultural history, one reflected
in the dilemmas of the individual. Problems for Tavernier are not just
temporal; they are spatial as well in belonging to a specific place, a
natural environment. He inevitably finds problems in history that have
parallels in the contemporary world, yet the linkage appears to exist
physically as well as culturally in space. For example, the racial
prejudice manifest in *Clean Slate* is evident in the European dress of
the Caucasian residents of the African town and the flowing cotton
gowns of the natives. The Whites sit at a table to dine; the natives on
the ground. The prejudice is inherent in the set. "In *Clean Slate* I think
you cannot separate Noiret from this little African town, he belonged
there. . . . When I want to describe, the settings are shown through
somebody's eyes piece by piece" (Jacobowitz et al. 1986, 67-68).

For *A Sunday in the Country*, Tavernier told the director of
photography, Bruno de Keyser, and the cameraman, Jean Harnois, that
the camera movements should precede or amplify the actions or
emotions; they should not be "functional" (Ciment et al. 1984, 7).
Before beginning filming, he had them watch Robert Altman's *Come
Back to the 5 & Dime, Jimmy Dean, Jimmy Dean* for the concept of

framing, for movements that linked the character to the surroundings and at the same time reinforced the rhythm of the movie. As a consequence, in the end-of-the-century movie, the characters as well as the uneventful Sunday incarnate Impressionism and communicate its pulse.

Tavernier found that his characters generally have depth because of the social explanations behind them. He added to them the political conflict between the Left and the Right in *The Clockmaker*. The victim in the novel is just a passerby; in the film, Bernard Descombes shoots a right-wing factory cop, a combination thug and informant. Though none of that political orientation is in Simenon's novel (there, the son runs away and kills so he can marry a young girl), *The Clockmaker* is dedicated to Jacques Prévert because Tavernier had wanted his film "to have that political freedom and that violence that Prévert had" (Jacobowitz et al. 1986, 66).

One of the most original ideas was Tavernier's use of a church clock's melody for the musical theme of the film. The clockmaker Descombes stops at one point to collect himself before the Church of Saint-Jean with its beautiful clock playing the theme. The composer Philippe Sarde composed the music around this theme of a thirteenth-century clock (Benoit 1974, 8). The rhythmic pulse of Tavernier's films accompanies the music; the camera movement, the montage, coincides with the musical rhythm. He used Eddy Mitchell's and Bill Evans's music for *A Week's Vacation*, Carla Bley's music for *Clean Slate*, and Gabriel Fauré's for *A Sunday in the Country*.

In 1986, Tavernier noted that what he liked about certain Hollywood films of the 1950s "was the use of landscapes and sets as dramatic elements, the characters' insertion in their environment" (Coursodon 1986, 23). By shooting *The Clockmaker* in Lyons, Tavernier returned to childhood memories and a familiar atmosphere. The large, high-ceilinged, somber rooms and the courtyards where you hear children practicing scales on the piano were all part of his own past (Demeure and Thirard 1974, 46).

In *Beatrice* Tavernier integrates the people into the settings, the light as well as the decor. From Jacques Tourneur, he learned that people speak differently to one another depending on the lighting (Douin 1988, 88). He tried to capture the light and violence of the countryside to reflect the violence of the feelings. There was a conscious effort by the photographer as well as himself to have the lighting correspond to the emotions of the characters. Beatrice seems linked to the vast landscape in which her medieval drama takes place. Her domineering father Cortemare arrives in darkness. Beatrice's room is filled with light until Cortemare sullies it by raping her.

In the Middle Ages, candles and torches remained fixed to avoid their being extinguished by drafts; they were expensive and utilized sparingly. As a consequence, to communicate the period, the cast ended up mounting stairs in darkness. The castle is lit only by candles; there are no fake film lights. This realism contributes to the feeling of history as lived versus a Hollywood set. Cameraman Bruno de Keyser, using a hand-held camera, is a Tavernier film crew regular (see *A Sunday in the Country*, and *'Round Midnight*), and presents us with a Middle Ages that appears real, a life lived in that period, rather than the picture postcard version of most historical films.

Similarly, the war in *Captain Conan* often takes place at night, never on a bright, sunny day. It is winter. The coldness of the war is communicated by this scenery and lighting and by the fall colors.

The solitude of Dale Turner (Dexter Gordon) in *'Round Midnight* is underscored as the camera remains on him after his initial solo performance, even though the famous jazz guitarist John McLaughlin is playing the following solo (figure 1). This camera sequence occurs twice during the film. Thus Dale becomes the isolated musician *par excellence*: alone on the screen while others play, a foreigner in Paris. The solitude and loneliness are visually felt, not just heard. The relationship between characters and their environment is underscored by use of a single light source in every scene and by the drab, cool colors Alexander Trauner used in the sets.

For *L. 627*, Tavernier's film about drug dealing, his co-scriptwriter was Michel Alexandre, a French police investigator who actually worked on the drug force. Tavernier met him through his son, Nils, who, after attempting suicide in 1985 because of drugs (Nils was 14), was put on a drug program, and, having recovered, now participates in youth education programs to prevent drugs. Nils himself plays the role of the cop Vincent. Charlotte Kady (Marie), who portrays a feisty woman cop on the drug team, used as a model an inspector Carole J. who had worked with Michel Alexandre on such a team. She borrowed her jeans, her leather jackets, and sexy T-shirts. Charlotte observed Carole at work to copy her gestures and her attitudes.

The choice of new actors for the film was also part of the everyday realism. None is a celebrated star that would place the viewers immediately in a world of fiction that is not their own. In order

Figure 1: Dale alone.   *'Round Midnight*

to shoot with a hidden camera, Tavernier needed actors who would not be recognized as they walked down the street. Thirty-five of the seventy actors were performing commercially for the first time. Didier Besace (Lulu) was selected for the principal role because he seems like an anonymous cop. The working conditions, reconstructed in the sixteenth sector, were exactly what he saw in Paris, two hundred meters from the Elysée Palace. All the policemen who saw the film noted how authentic the sets were.

Daddy Nostalgia is done for the wide screen to dramatize the larger social context that lies beneath the family drama and its lack of communication. The use of cinemascope permits a long tracking shot to capture the father's longing for the real success he never had in a gaze over the edge of the villa's garden to the sea below. Another long tracking shot encircles Caroline as she sits alone on the beach after learning of her father's imminent death. Their solitude is set into this landscape by the use of scope.

In *The Judge and the Assassin*, Joseph Vacher was the historical late nineteenth-century sadistic assassin tracked down and condemned to death by a judge. Inspired by the discovery of an unpublished synopsis filled with historical notations, most of which Tavernier kept,

Figure 2: The Factory.   *Life and Nothing But*

filling in with fragments of dialogue from letters of Mirabeau, Valles, or Zola, Tavernier handled both vast scenic displays as well as intimate scenes placed in their cultural context. The savage and immense landscape of the Vivarais matches the lecherous and murderous emotions of Bouvier. Streets seem inhabited, customs of the period, because, unexplained, they pull us into a reality of the times. A ballad is sung in the streets to express the frustrations of people just as the Internet is used today. Prisons and hospitals are of their time, with their starkness and cruelties unmodified by the sterilized twentieth century and the American Civil Liberties Union.

In *Life and Nothing But*, to communicate the grimness of war, to get the black, white, and blue of a landscape devastated by war, "we used a technical process to take the green out of the picture" (Jaehne 1990, 11). The setting of the abandoned factory with huge dysfunctional machines is used to communicate power and simultaneously show the inhumanity of power (figure 2). We understand why power is disparaged when we learn that this munitions factory was not bombed by the Germans because of a collaborator, the father of the heroine.

Use of the steadicam has permitted Tavernier to connect the

characters to their environment and yet communicate their freedom from frozen forms. It tends to confer a strange lightness to the pictures, an absence of clashes that permit one to climb or descend stairs, run or stop as one desires. As a consequence, the sound is direct and the camera very mobile. Traveling shots always limit Tavernier: the rails are never long enough because he seeks to join the characters as well as the decor in the movement of the film.

> The steadicam gave me a style of production that continually put people back into the setting and pursued the characters while they looked at one another, watched each other. That permitted me then to locate them continually in relation to one another. . . . I could use the steadicam in a new way. Until now it has almost always been used for shots aimed at having a certain effect, whereas I wanted to use it to give an immense degree of freedom to the actors, to be able to go everywhere without appearing to do so. (Cèbe 1981, 29-30)

What interests him about the steadicam is that you do not develop a center for the compositions and give instead a feeling of floating up in the air, reflecting Tavernier's attempt to decipher a terrain that does not have a stable base (Ciment et al, 1984, 6).

Everyday Objects

In *The Clockmaker*, Michel fixes the instruments that order our lives, yet the immediate effect of Michel's fixing the clock in the restaurant where he eats regularly is to make him late for dinner. He himself works on his own schedule like a true artisan and, when he was younger, even took his son to work with him. Clocks, as objects, play almost a contrapuntal role to the events Michel has to try to comprehend for the first time in his life, namely the reason why his son would kill a man. To collect his thoughts, he goes to the cathedral that houses the most famous clock in France, where every movement is regulated. Nothing about what he is trying to understand seems regulated, yet everyone is trying to make the murder fit into a pre-established order, to make it work, justifying it as a murder of passion to avoid the true political reasons for revolt and making it fit into the acceptable mode that does not criticize the *status quo*.

Michel is having an embarrassing, clichéd conversation about his son with a journalist when he stops before a strange little object discovered in his son's room—a crude machine for making matches; it reminds him of the funny story about his great uncle who made matches illegally and got caught because the phosphorus he had picked up on the nails in the shoe soles made sparks on the pavement when he walked. The journalist immediately becomes less aggressive in his manner and more sympathetic towards Descombes (Bion 1984, 62-63). This everyday object plays an even more important role in the reunion of father and son, as it provides a perspective of revolt within the family, even on a minor scale, that goes back generations, impugning the social system over a much longer period of time.

In *A Week's Vacation*, the depressed heroine Laurence often looks out her window across the street at an unknown old woman knitting, reading, or just staring into space. At the end of the film, the shot reappears, but the window is shuttered. Laurence's friend Anne admits she had never noticed the woman until that week. "One day, she was gone. Perhaps she moved. She never had any visitors." The detail reveals a quite different sensitivity in Laurence and Anne, and the spectators realize that Laurence knows that she undoubtedly died, whereas Anne prefers to dismiss her absence with an unconcerned social excuse.

Emotion is communicated with details, not great events.

Meals

Tavernier often shows people eating together because, "given modern life, the most interesting things, the things that matter, are said during meals" (Bion 1984, 51). Lyons is renowned for its gastronomy, and appropriately, *The Clockmaker* opens with a meal in a place called the Restaurant Chauvin where the clientele defends the old versus the new. In the script, Michel Descombes says confidently, "Hell, for me, is paved with fast food restaurants, wimpy bars, and self-service diners. Can you imagine, an eternity of hormone-injected chickens and grilled steak with *herbes de Provence*" (Tavernier 1974, 10). His son's act of murder will wrench him from this secure frame of reference, that of social definition. The everyday meal serves to reveal the anguish felt by the father. Later while all the friends eat heartily, he barely touches his food. Tavernier affirmed in 1974 that

it is essential to make films rooted in a culture, a society, and not imitations without ties to any country. French scenario writers who imitate American cinema show they have understood nothing about the original which was profoundly rooted, if not in a precise reality, at least in a tradition that was as literary, moral, religious, and philosophical, as social. (Braucourt 1974, 64)

Tavernier moved the setting from an American small-town to Lyons, which is the epitome of an industrialized city and has the values of mass society that the son Bernard rejects. One of the posters in his room is entitled "Polluted France." In contrast, the former housekeeper Madeleine's simple house in the suburbs, with its ramshackle yard—Madeleine is nonexistent in the novel—stands for the values Bernard and his father like. We are told, however, that the authorities are planning to tear down the house to build a hospital, one more example where the individual is replaced by institutional concrete. "Ultimately the solidarity of [the father] Descombes and [the son] Bernard depends on the added dimension of their common antipathy for the surrounding culture" (Magretta and Magretta 1979, 281).

In *Captain Conan* (1996) the conflict between the regular military and Conan's band of guerrillas is communicated by the meals they eat. Whereas the officers dine in the formal, regulated style dictated by the rules of French cuisine, no matter how meager the fare may be, the guerrillas gorge themselves on what they have stolen, with much better wines, and in no style whatsoever. Both scenes are perfectly realistic, engaging the spectators directly in the conflict between the two.

Everyman

Philippe Noiret's great asset is his unegotistical nature, which makes him appear as everyman, someone who is known and believable. "If any actor in the world can be a 'leading player' or even a 'star' and still retain a fundamentally anonymous quality," interviewer Joseph Hurley notes, "that actor is very probably Philippe Noiret" (1982, 167). Trained as an actor, he has played over 120 roles. He is one of very few actors who have worked with Italy's most prestigious directors (his role in *The Postman* most recently), as well as with Cukor and Hitchcock, to say nothing of major French directors. Noiret has the ability to communicate the ordinary man of the street in a very powerful manner. In 1990, Tavernier said, "I resist the heroism of the individual. My personae are never heroic, although they may be admirable" (Jaehne 1990, 13).

And like the everyman of the American B-movies he so admired, his characters are neither all good nor all bad. This dual nature is what engages the spectators to comprehend rather than judge the characters. Though they judge at first, upon discovering the opposing side of the character, they must squarely face the prejudice that caused the judgment and question its absolute nature. In *L.627* the policewoman Carole is bitten by a dealer (figure 3), but the undercover cop Lulu becomes so mad he almost kills one of the drug dealers being held in his office (figure 4). As the spectators try to understand the character, they are inevitably led to the social background that prompted the bad side to develop—and sometimes the good.

In the hierarchical structure, the winner is rewarded. Tavernier has a great time satirizing the consequences in *The Daughter of D'Artagnan* when the musketeers, grown older since they championed the distressed in *The Three Musketeers*, throw the fine art of swordplay to the winds, and instead use cheating, pushing, and shoving to win. Upon losing his sword to a swipe from his opponent, Aramis, the perfectionist in the art, pulls a pistol and shoots western-style—a marvelous satire of modern politics.

Prostitution and theft are equally good ways to win within the hierarchical structure. In *Let Joy Reign Supreme*, a man hanged for theft has his boots stolen from him before he has even been cut down. The system does not impact just the peasants and the poor. Even the royal physician and the Comte de Horn steal. Where economic value guarantees a superior position in the hierarchy, even people are stolen (kidnapped) by the Regent's men and sold to work in America. The Regent, a symbol of debauchery, nonetheless tried to solve the economic problems of his time, wrote music (some of which Tavernier used in the film), and encouraged the sciences. He was neither all good nor all bad.

In *Beatrice*, François de Cortemare's blatant vulgarity, his gratuitous brutality to his own son and daughter, and the way he defiles all that is sacred and pure makes us detest his violence and willed self-destruction, but his own self-hatred makes him appear human. He hates himself so much that he runs into a burning house and has to be pulled out. Later, he even shows his daughter where to kill him. Simplifying the story as a struggle between good and evil is too easy and superficial, especially since the obviously good daughter ends up murdering the father, with our approval. We even desire it.

In *The Judge and the Assassin* actor Galabru depicts a character

Figure 3: Carole bitten by a dealer. *L.627*

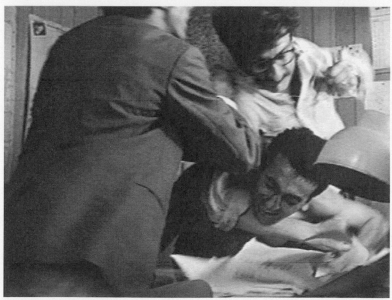

Figure 4: Lulu beats a dealer. *L.627*

torn by the social injustices to which he has been subjected, expressing
the concerns of not only his age, but ours. Reviewer Stanley
Kauffmann rightly calls Galabru's "maniacally transfigured murderer
a performance that comes straight from the heart of Dostoevskian
torment," comparing his outbursts of ecstasy to those of Falconetti in
Dreyer's *Jeanne d'Arc* (Kauffmann 1982, 24). Fundamentally simple
in his peasant nature with a family and religious tradition, unsure of
himself after being rejected by his fiancée, he seeks a visible, public
renown to compensate; in search of recognition, he plays the role of a
social hero far beyond his natural abilities, using his war
commendations as a spring board to excuse his numerous rapes and
murders.

In *L.627*, the drug film, the characters are, as in all Tavernier
films, neither clearly good guys or bad guys, but a human mixture. The
cops use too much brutality on the drug dealers who reciprocate
(figures 3 and 4); the drug dealers show as much human concern and
sensitivity for others as do the best of the cops. The spectator cannot
easily take side whole-heartedly for one individual against another. The
drug addicts are clearly a result of social ills and the drug team is
underequipped and understaffed.

Philippe Torreton won the *César* (the French equivalent of an
Oscar) for best actor in *Captain Conan* (1996), undoubtedly in part
because he portrays an ordinary man (he worked in his family's little
shop selling sewing goods before the war) who leads his men on
extraordinary exploits in war, and then becomes a nobody again when
peace is declared. Of course he does not become a nobody very
successfully. He succeeds very well, however, in convincing us of the
reality of both his careers. An everyman, regardless.

Marginals

The Clockmaker was inspired by a 1954 Simenon novel, *The
Watchmaker of Everton*, set in America in the 1930s, about immigrants
who were not completely at home in their new society. Simenon had
captured "a certain atmosphere and loneliness in the American society,
of somebody who cannot adapt," says Tavernier of the novel
(Jacobowitz et al. 1986, 65). "But I didn't want to do an American
film, and I tried to transpose it to my native city, Lyons" and to a
different period, that of France in the late 1960s.

Marginals permit a director to satirize social prejudices, having caught the spectators in the apparent realism of the setting. Bouvier, in *The Judge and the Assassin*, is such a marginal. He was sufficiently educated to know how to read and write, yet excluded from all levels of society: the army, the family, religious institutions, and even the asylum. Numerous aspects of the frozen form are satirized thereby.

(1) Privilege before the law, or hierarchical class structure. Another judge has just returned from Cochin-Chine (now Vietnam) assuring Judge Rousseau that Bouvier will not be found insane because he is poor; and this is what happens. Those in power—the judge and magistrate—become more and more absurd and unjust, as they progress ever more sharply towards an untenable absolute position that tolerates no differences of opinion, much as the extremist groups in the United States—or elsewhere—today.

(2) Bourgeois sense of supremacy. Anti-Semitism, intensified because of the Dreyfus affair taking place during the same historical period, is embodied by the bourgeois prejudices of Mme. Rousseau, the Judge's mother, who refuses to serve soup to vagrants who would not sign a petition against Dreyfus. The anti-Semitism is underscored ironically during the magistrate's suicide scene by the music of Offenbach. When the anarchists burst in on the Royalists in the final scene, the judge and mother flee to a nook beneath a poster advertising an anti-Semitic newspaper.

(3) Language as cliché. Bouvier's use of language subverts the order of things. He takes clichés to control the poor, whether those of the Church and sainthood or the politicians and educators and misinterprets them or interprets the metaphors literally. "And you're like the Bishop who burned Joan of Arc!"—rightfully questioning the Judge's condemnation while blasphemously comparing himself to Joan of Arc; or "You know I have a weakness for earthly angels," that is, the twelve- to fifteen-year-old youths he killed and sodomized; or "Truly God has used me and such a Calvary must be avenged." From the mouth of Bouvier, the clichéd phrases of justice are exposed as nothing but that, clichés hiding prejudices.

Several of Tavernier's films deal with the ruptures that occur in personal relationships when an individual is totally immersed in his work. The Commander Dellaplane, in *Life and Nothing But*, fails to establish bonds with Irene because he is so intent on his job. In *L.627* the family life of police officer Lulu suffers in the same way. An amateur videographer, he shoots more footage of drug busts than he

does of his own daughter. Though they are not strictly marginals in
society, they become estranged in a similar manner. Tavernier himself
very much identifies with these characters. "When I make a film, I
sometimes risk hurting the people who live with me because the film
takes a devouring place in my life" (Bonneville 1993, 15).

Periods in Transition

Tavernier's best films are all set in epochs during which something was
coming to an end, such as *The Clockmaker* (1968), *Beatrice* (1500s),
the pre-war films—*The Judge and the Assassin*, *A Sunday in the
Country*, and the post-war films—*Life and Nothing But*, *Captain
Conan*. Whereas the American setting of the Simenon novel on which
The Clockmaker was based dealt with the depression years, Tavernier
deals with the years of unrest that preceded and followed the May 1968
aborted revolt. The period is defined in the film as one in which the
individual is suffocated by the attempt to maintain a sense of comfort
at all costs. ("On étouffe dans ce putain de pays, avec ce climat de
lâcheté, cette espèce de confort satisfait que l'on entretient par tous les
moyens.") The son of the clockmaker Descombes, Bernard rejects the
crime-of-passion motive that his attorney wants to use to justify the
murder; he insists instead on the general injustice prevailing in society.
He killed because "I didn't want the same ones to come out ahead." By
insisting that the truth be told, "Bernard exposes as an ideological
weapon society's humanitarian pretenses. Society would like nothing
better than a sympathetic psychiatric report or a crime of passion plea,
for it could then show its leniency through a reduced sentence and
avoid troubling questions of conscience" (Bates 1985, 32).

     This film, along with Tavernier's next two, *Let Joy Reign Supreme*
and *The Judge and the Assassin*, form a trilogy for him. All three deal
with moments of French history and different social classes ("the
average male of the twentieth century, the aristocrat of the eighteenth
century and the bourgeois of the nineteenth century") that reflect the
struggle between justice and injustice in the society of the time as well
as in the main character, a consequence of the hierarchical power
structure, regardless of the century. *Let Joy Reign Supreme* treats the
reign of Philippe d'Orléans after the death of Louis XIV until Louis
XV comes of age. The era of decadence shows the seeds of revolution
already in place. History has always interested Tavernier because of the

light it sheds on our contemporary world. Tavernier has the ability to make us feel as though we are part of the period, not onlookers. The historical texture comes alive—something Tavernier claims to have learned from Hugo, Zola, Shakespeare, and the great French theatrical director Jean Vilar. Because of these characteristics, Tavernier's historical films stand out from films dealing with everyday life (*L. 627, Deathwatch, Spoiled Children, A Week's Vacation,* and *Fresh Bait*—all of which would be seen as good films if not compared with the historical ones).

The setting after World War I of *Life and Nothing But* places the spectators in a situation where sociocultural clichés of heroism dictate our response. Then Tavernier strips each cliché to the bone one by one, including that of "The Unknown Soldier" as a glory and justification for the innumerable deaths in war. Tavernier does not make a big deal of the cliché, but quietly presents ordinary, realistic details that strip it of its meaning more profoundly than any argument could. Let's consider these heroic clichés one by one.

(1) Soldiers who fought in a war are heroes. The Arc de Triomphe with the tomb of the unknown soldier is undoubtedly the supreme monument representing French victory. Tavernier's entire cinematic approach, the use of cinemascope for intimate stories, defies the notion of heroism by continually taking in more than the individual. Tavernier reminded his cameraman of John Ford's economical use of the close-up specifically in *She Wore a Yellow Ribbon*. Using the wide shots of cinemascope for an intimate story "seemed appropriate, because the audacious use of space would emphasize the historical dimensions" (Jaehne 1990, 13).[1] Then he shows us the attempts to discover the body of an unknown soldier that, though unidentifiable, is guaranteed not to be German, or American, or Moroccan, etc. The local gossip that comes out in the process makes the whole endeavor appear ridiculous.

(2) The military commands respect and awe. Most of the military procedures appear to be nothing but a sham. Soldiers are given an identity based on a broken cup or other everyday object identified by a family member or beloved.

(3) The upper classes and politicians in particular deserve the utmost respect and they are powerful. Irene de Courtil's father-in-law is shown to have collaborated with the Germans so that his munitions factory alone has been spared. His family nickname is "Pony," something we discover along with Major Dellaplane (Noiret) after his fit of jealousy that occurs when he imagines Irene to be speaking on the

telephone to a lover called "Pony."

(4) What politicians say is important. Dellaplane counts 350,000 missing in battle, but since the French had more dead than the Germans, the official number was much lower to prove the French victory. France's 1.4 million dead are referred to as an "eloquent record." As an illustration of the "French lie," the political fraud that was current at the time, Tavernier noted that Stanley Kubrick's *Paths of Glory* was forbidden in France for fifteen years because it showed a French general shooting a French soldier for insubordination (Jaehne 1990, 10). The blatant lies made by politicians to maintain power are exposed.

(5) Entrepreneurship is eminently respectable. The sculptor Mercadot is delighted by all the dead: he has so many commissions for monuments to them that he is becoming rich. With 300 sculptors for 35,000 towns needing monuments, he considers it a veritable "Renaissance." Another entrepreneur offers to search for the dead beloved for a fee—but never produces a body.

(6) Men run the world. Irene accuses Dellaplane of belonging to a club that creates wars—a "club" because women are excluded. Alice is fired as a teacher because the former teacher is a soldier now returned from war.

(7) "Liberté, Égalité, Fraternité," the great French motto. But racism is manifest in the relegation of French-Africans fighting the war to their own table at the local restaurant serving as a mess hall and they are "preferred" for searching the mine fields.

This general critique of social prejudices is never merely destructive; Tavernier chooses historical moments in transition precisely to show new relationships being born and discovered—always engendered by feelings born of human contact rather than by the frozen social forms that pre-existed. Thus Dellaplane and Irene bond, as do the schoolteacher and a young artist.

The Middle Ages appealed to Tavernier because it was a pre-psychological period when emotions existed in brutal purity. No romantic sentimentalism disguised them. Many of Tavernier's films dwell on feelings, on the way they affect our lives, rather than the intellectual abilities around which most French films revolve. The feelings are not the petty jealousies of the French *ménage à trois*. Tavernier's kind of feelings are those that explain profound human bonding, or estrangement. Today, civilization "has taught us to dissimulate feelings. Masks have been placed on social and human

Figure 5: The Acrobat.   *A Sunday in the Country*

relationships. But some of these masks are cracking" (Lequeux 1988, 23). Tavernier is partial to historical sets because they "underscore the essential changeless aspect of social institutions and human relations; the repetition of the present reflected in the past destroys the mask with which civilization has hidden them. In *Beatrice*, Tavernier's third historical film, this one set in the Middle Ages, the lord of the manor is anything but a model of lordship, yet he still has the authority to behave as master. In an interview, Tavernier observed he does not understand people who work based on relationships of power.

The year 1905 was a time of transition, the end of the nineteenth with its horse and buggy and the beginning of the twentieth or the age of automobiles. Set in that period, *A Sunday in the Country* deals with the complexities of forging a family, or a work of art, a career. These being dynamic processes, the phenomenon of an older era permits the perspective of distance to highlight problems we do not see in a present in which we are involved. We are presented with a family gathering, a meeting of persons who have spent years together and yet we feel there is no real communication among them. In Pierre Bost's book, on which the film is based, the father talks throughout of taking his daughter to a café by the lake, but never does. Tavernier had already

written the scene where the father does just that before he discovered
that it was not in the book. For him, the momentary contact between
the two is an essential ingredient. There will be a similar scene in
Daddy Nostalgia. But in *A Sunday in the Country* the daughter makes
the father feel that he should have continued to paint the picture of the
acrobat (figure 5). That picture she will not sell: it is filled with
emotion, with human beings. In the book, she leaves without the
contact ever having occurred, a much more tragic family than the one
Tavernier depicts.

September 10, 1918, the date when *Captain Conan* begins, is
approaching the end of World War I. The energy and the purpose the
soldiers might have displayed in 1914 are long gone. The only ones
who still have it, we discover, are Conan and his band, men who,
thanks to the war, have discovered an elevated sense of existence
unknown to them before. They are only sure they really exist when
killing, like Bouvier in *The Judge and the Assassin*. Again, the distance
between that moment of warfare reflects on today's guerrilla warfare
around the world. It would appear as sacrilege to blatantly question the
heroism of guerrillas fighting in numerous little wars around the world
today. *Captain Conan* does just that, especially for those taking place
in the Balkans.

Tavernier's treatment of contemporary subjects underscores the
power of historical subjects to engage the spectator by generating
parallels. The contemporary subject simply appears as the reality we
already know. The historical subjects appear to be about a different
world, yet we discover uneasy parallels with our own world and look
at a familiar reality from an outside point of view that shatters the walls
built by habit.

Spoiled Children deals with landlords who exploit the tenants by
raising rents unmercifully. When a large number of those tenants are
suffering from high unemployment rates in the country generally, the
heartlessness of the already wealthy landlord seems especially unjust.
Déjà vu, déjà su. Tavernier was, himself, president of the Tenants'
Legal committee of a building he lived in for several years and
experienced many of the events first hand. But in the film, we do not
particularly change our opinion of any one individual nor of the general
situation between the start and the end of the film. The film lacks the
depth that the doubling of an event distant in time brings to a story.
Though Bernard Rougerie (played by Michel Piccoli) is writing a film
script that develops like the film we are seeing, more or less, this fails

to do more than reiterate the reality shown. It does not engage the viewers to discover a relationship between their own present and that of the film as does a historical setting. With the contemporary period, there is no act of discovery, of discomfort, but rather a "yeah, we know" reaction on behalf of the viewers. A story of America's great depression would have had as much relevance and would have engaged the spectator creatively—but that setting would not have been French, something Tavernier holds very dear. *Spoiled Children* suffers particularly from this lack of depth, thereby verging on the polemic instead of a universal truth about hierarchical power structures and exploitation. Tavernier had wanted to avoid this pitfall and admitted that he was too close to the problem.

Historical Fidelity versus Storytelling

In *Beatrice* Tavernier refuses to explain to us the role of the woman who is either a saint or crazy, because in the Middle Ages people would not have needed an explanation: it was a phenomenon of the culture that needed none. The Christian religion and sorcery co-existed, with the pope practicing both at the time. Similarly, death was pervasive. France was just beginning to recover from a black plague that had reduced the population by a third in many towns. When a baby died, its existence was not even inscribed in the ledgers of the parish.

This use of the cultural habits of a time without explanation to the contemporary viewers has a dual effect. On the one hand, it convinces them of the authenticity of the story being told and on the other, creates a breach in the walls of the current hierarchical structure. Suddenly the walls do not seem so solid, so closed, because we know that custom does not make sense by today's knowledge. This is one of the ways in which Tavernier uses realism itself to question frozen forms. Like it, numerous others violate conventional narrative concepts.

In short, Tavernier uses realism to engage the viewers in a familiar world, then pulls the rug of habit from beneath them, leaving them questioning their own habits and prejudices as well as those of their society.

Notes

1. Commenting on the script, Tavernier made the following remark of the restaurant scene: "This room is the description of a social class that no longer exists in France. And it is part of the theme of the film: the reconstruction, the effort, along with the surrounding dramas and individual conflicts, incorporated into a collective vision. All that stands in opposition to the ideology of the individualist hero. The characters are inserted into their context and the emotion is part of the general problem. Philippe Noiret is rarely alone on the screen. The camera always brings us back to the next table or to someone passing. He is a character rarely cut off from his context and from the world about him—the way John Ford filmed" (Tavernier 1990, 26).

3

Emotion Instead of Plot

While Tavernier engages the spectators in a realistic, familiar world, he questions causal development and the significance of events and characters by a series of techniques that simultaneously fracture the frozen cultural forms. One of the disruptive characteristics of his films that leads the viewers to join up with the film's action is Tavernier's violation of linear storyline. His sense of progression in a film precludes the usual realistic omniscient author. What makes his realism different comes from staging principles such as "never using a counter-shot on persons one is following" (B.B., D.R.-B. 1992, 59).

> I try to make the movement of a film coincide with that of its characters, have the same rhythmic changes, the same hesitations, that things be discovered at the same time as the characters discover them.
>
> That demands a structure which sometimes appears groping, especially during the first fifteen minutes. I have always had beginnings that were haphazard, zigzagging, even uncertain. . . . The dramatic conflict and especially the reasons for this conflict appear later. . . .
>
> Aurenche taught me to write freely, to develop a scene for the pleasure of it, letting the characters lead, without knowing where one is going. (Tavernier, *Qu'est-ce qu'on attend,* 1993, 43)

Qu'est-ce qu'on attend is a journal Tavernier kept while filming *L.627.* The searching for relationships along with the characters means the story cannot be developed causally, as taught in English composition or screen-writing manuals. Not finding the usual clues, the

viewers must go along with the action they see. The ideological
consequences usually violate accepted cultural prejudices.

Though based on the English novel by David Compton, *The
Continuous Katherine Mortenhoe*, Tavernier's *Deathwatch* goes a step
beyond the book. The story of the making of a film within a film, it
serves as a commentary on many of Tavernier's principles. The
futuristic science-fiction thesis assumes two things: that science has
obliterated death from disease and that a camera can be implanted into
a person's eye, preventing sleep, denying privacy and secrecy. Whereas
the novel only tells of the consequences, the film becomes another eye
watching the eye, engendering a self-commentary on film as spectacle
or storyline. The story was supposed to be the appeal to the television
viewers of watching an individual die who, because of a disease, knows
death will come too soon. A television producer arranges to give a
well-known writer, played by Romy Schneider (shortly before her own
real death in 1982), an overdose of drugs to induce the symptoms of
illness and thereby convince her of her impending death. Then she
would be followed by the camera and saved theatrically at the last
moment by taking her off the drugs. Produced seventeen years before
the prying eyes of the paparazzi instigated the events prior to Princess
Diana's death, the film seemed too gloomy and did not enjoy a
commercial success. In 1997, the science-fiction element appears
considerably reduced, little more than a metaphor for the reality of the
inquisitional eyes of a media turned rabid by the lack of war as a topic.

The film goes beyond an indictment of the media; it questions plot
itself. Literally watching the plot unfold, it shows plot as self-
referential and self-destructive:

(1) Harvey Keitel (Roddy in the film), playing the television
reporter, becomes personally attached to Romy Schneider as Katherine
and, discovering that his eyes are making a public spectacle of their
intimacies, throws away the light required to keep his camera eyes
charged rather than reduce the death of someone he respects and
admires to a mere spectacle. Roddy's camera eyes reference Tavernier
himself. Roddy discovers he has a responsibility for what he films and
shows to the public. The guilt he feels at having transgressed that
responsibility justifies his subsequent blindness. Tavernier never
commits irresponsible acts of the sort, always conscious of the social
implications of what he projects onto the screen.

(2) In the film, Katherine commits suicide rather than allow the
television producers to control the plot, thus transforming them into

murderers—as the paparazzi were to appear upon Princess Diana's death—rather than gods controlling spectacle. This self-referencing on the part of both the writer and the director is compounded by Katherine's profession as a writer who generates novels via computer, a computer that produces pulp romances, rejecting any used plot developments or endings. When her computer refuses to accept one of her favorite conclusions, she experiences the frustration all humans do when confronted with a computer that does not understand their wishes. Her decision to commit suicide by taking an overdose of her medication is in part a self-vindication. Her computer had accepted as original the conclusion for a work-in-progress: "Amy, alone on beach, appears nude, watching." But can she terminate the actual plot against her in an original manner? As she says to Roddy, "Aren't many ways out any more." The dramatic death scene has become too clichéd to be an acceptable ending. For her own end and that of the film, she rejects both the drama the television series demanded and prevents the film's audience from having the sense of a dramatic conclusion by turning the plot backwards on both the television producers and the audience that has sat for two hours in anticipation of watching her death. Her suicide, her moment of death, is not even shown in the film.

In Tavernier's films no analysis of sentiments attempts to explain them away in a causal manner. The emotions between two people just are; they exist for their own sake. To reveal the emotions as the truly human force, Tavernier avoids pulling strings or using the clichéd: *Life and Nothing But*, as one reviewer noted, is a *film policier* without a cop, a war without a battle, a love story without a kiss" (Le Morvan 1989, 25). In his quest for mood and emotion, Tavernier shuns strict progression, seeking counterpoint, a melody with a counterpoint behind, or a variation, as though one is experiencing moments of a life, "a construction closer to impressionism, closer to music than to a stage play" (Dempsey 1987, 10).

Tavernier observed that in *Life and Nothing But* the only place where there is a beginning, middle, and end "is the subplot of the government wanting to find [its] unknown soldier—what I call the 'official story'" (Jaehne 1990, 12). Intentionally structured along the lines of American screwball comedy, it is propelled by misunderstandings that hinder the romance, misunderstandings fostered by class differences and individual purpose. Whereas Irene's husband comes from a family of collaborators, if not downright traitors, Major Dellaplane is accused of being a Dreyfusard and seeks justice with a passion. Whereas Dellaplane pursues his statistics as a truth, a reality he can grasp, Irene wants basically to find out whether she is married or widowed, so she can get on with her own life. We encounter a series of tableaux that have little to do with finding an unknown soldier.

None of these tableaux deals with a great event, the decisive battle for instance. Whereas most films that claim to be against war are a "display of pageantry about some great event," Tavernier concentrates on either the causes or the effects of war, the latter in this film, because they permit you "to portray the human dimension instead of a heroic ideal that does not fit humanity" (Jaehne 1990, 11). The effects of war tend to reveal the social prejudices that brought it about as irrelevant, leaving open the development of something new in the future.

A Week's Vacation has no plot. Laurence, a professor at a French college, experiences a major crisis of self-doubt about her profession. A friend who is a doctor gets her a week off from teaching. Encountering various people during the week, she returns to work at the end of the week. However her teacher-friend Anne leaves. This is not "a plot." There is no cause and effect, no linear development, no event.

The action in the drug dealing *L. 627* is not subject to a given plot. Having no plot or classical construction (beginning, middle, and end), the spectators do not at first know with whom to identify. The changing points of view also disorient the spectator. All is geared to prevent "adhesion to an ideology" (B.B. et al. 1992, 58). The movement is a matter of quick takes to communicate the mental and moral energy of the principal character." In the montage, they used "no fades, no dissolves" (Bonneville 1993, 16). The dialogues themselves are "rapid and nervous" (Bonneville 1993, 16).

Within each scene of *Daddy Nostalgia*, the motion seems stilled; the sense of motion comes from the sequencing of these short scenes. Tavernier himself referred to the structure of the film as suggesting a kind of diary. The short scenes, not action, generate the drama that is felt within the spectator. The montage "is not dictated by plot, but by emotion" (Paletz 1992, 45). For instance, Caroline descends from a bus to visit her father in the hospital. In front of her, a young woman is greeted by the arms of her lover. They move off together while Caroline takes a lonely stroll on the pier. Only later do we realize that her father was never there to take her in his arms as a child, either; and here she is running to his deathbed. The scenes at home show first

Figure 6: "Not now. Go see Nanny."   *Daddy Nostalgia*

one parent talking with Caroline, rarely both—and then there is always an argument. Then a scene follows showing the other, often the mother, in solitary activity or thought, such as the shot where she is alone in front of the television watching the pope, or lying in bed, alone with her rosary. There is no talk of estrangement and solitude in the film, yet the spectator is haunted by those feelings at the film's end.

Tavernier uses seemingly trivial details to evoke past memories in brief flashbacks. In *Daddy Nostalgia* we learn about the family past in flashbacks to Caroline's childhood where she is seen dressed up for an adult party. She tries to get her father's attention by writing him a poem and delivering it to him at the party. She is greeted with the "Not-now, go-see-Nanny" rejection (figure 6). One of these brief flashbacks occurs just before their final fling when he asks to read her next script and she observes, "That's the first time you've ever asked to read anything I wrote." The child's immense loneliness and neglect are felt, heart-rendering. The film is about emotion and caring, not plot or events. The lines of the theme song are picked up in the flashbacks. The father had "an airline ticket to romantic places," while Caroline remained alone with a Nanny. In Caroline's Paris apartment, there is "a telephone that rings but who's to answer?"

A detail as trivial as the combination lock on the father's briefcase is equally poignant. Alone in the kitchen where the daughter is cleaning up, the father fiddles with it and notes: "The date of my birth, the date of my marriage, and the date of my maiden voyage." The date of his daughter's birth, the same year as his voyage, is obviously inconsequential, though he easily remembers details of the voyage. When she reminds him that that was also the year of her birth, he bluntly confesses that she was a "bloody accident." His quasi-honesty mixed with his blatant egotism give him a truly human quality that makes him an interesting, seemingly real person. With nothing heroic or extraordinary about any of them, the family nonetheless retains our close attention. No violence or shouting is needed to communicate very deep human pain, the kind of pain no doctor can cure and that is not explained by any one event.

Flashbacks in Tavernier communicate feeling or foster comprehension, not as explanations or justifications for subsequent events. In *The Clockmaker*, the enigma to be solved is not the traditional one of finding out who the culprit is, and only momentarily that of his capture. The plot is concerned rather with the motives for the crime, leaving the spectator with a disturbing social problem that is not resolved when the "case is closed" (Demeure and Thirard 1974, 41). In the original Simenon novel for *The Clockmaker*, Dave's search for an explanation of his son's act involves "the interweaving of memory and introspection with the present action" (Magretta and Magretta 1979, 278). Instead of resorting to a literal transposition using flashbacks and voice-overs, Tavernier has Michel's understanding come, not from the past, but from the actions as they unfold in the present. A lot of this is made possible by the re-creation of the role of the police. In the novel, the police also show a sympathetic indulgence for the father, but it is not set up as a countercurrent that ends in total lack of comprehension as in Tavernier.

Counterpoint Rather Than Causal Development

In *The Clockmaker*, the film is organized as two opposing emotional or psychological developments that occur simultaneously, generating a tension that grabs the spectator. The father's search for comprehension of the truth and his own self-discovery are reflected in the concrete itinerary he follows: along the streets of Lyons, the train trip to

Figure 7: "Keep the change."   *The Clockmaker*

Saint-Brieuc, the plane flight home. Each trip corresponds to a precise realization on his part. The transformation is made manifest by the change in the father Descombes' attitude towards the law. As Michel Descombes' respect for the law disintegrates, his communication with and understanding of his son increases.

The disintegration is shown on several levels. First is Michel's respect for a red stoplight; in the end of the film he does not even look to see if a car is coming. Michel's response to authoritative figures changes similarly. When the police first arrive, he is most submissive and respectful. This attitude ceases when the hired henchmen break his shop windows and he and his friend settle the score physically rather than reporting it to the police. The police chief Guiboud, like Michel, has a son with whom he does not communicate too well. The complex relationship between the two provides the core of the dramatic action, for it slowly becomes evident that Guiboud, like the attorney and the reporters, is on the side of the rigid conventions that are stifling individuals. We know the end of Michel's respect has occurred definitively when he leaves the police chief at the restaurant, telling him to "keep the change" as though he were nothing but a waiter (figure 7).

Only because of the crime do the father and son come to discover how much alike they are and begin to have something to say to one another for the first time in their lives. As one reviewer notes, "[t]here have been scores of films and plays about the generation gap; this film about generation affinity seems more searching and true" (Gilliatt 1976, 51). The son is surprised to find that his father has the same contempt he has for the law's excuse of passion as a motive. He first discovers the likeness before the examining magistrate. He calls his attorney's explanation of passion a stupidity. The attorney appeals to the father to help him talk to his son. "What do you expect him to say to me?" asks the son. The father quietly looks at his son and replies: "Nothing." At the trial, the father also announces that he is completely in agreement with his son. The scene that clinches the relationship is the story the father tells the son when he visits him in prison, a story he had never before told him: during the war, a general had ordered him to go back into a burning house to retrieve the general's violin, threatening him with a court-martial when he refused. Descombes hauled off and hit the general, feeling much better afterward, but haunted throughout the remainder of the war that he would be picked up and court-martialed. Bernard is obviously all ears, responding with a big, warm smile. The scene closes with Descombes' story of how he and his friend Antoine had chased the two thugs, who damaged his clock shop after the Razon murder, beat them up, and tossed them into the Saône River. If *The Clockmaker* begins with the father's total incomprehension of his son's act, he seems to have complete understanding of it and the son at the end. In the prison's visitor room he arranges to care for the child (Bernard has twenty years of prison to do; his pregnant girlfriend five), much to Bernard's pleasure, fot he thinks his father had been a good father to him. Descombes finds conversation with his son natural and easy for the first time. Neither one seems alone, though they are physically separated.

Composed of oppositions and contrasts, *A Sunday in the Country* leaps from one set to the next: the young versus the old; the dull bourgeois son and the arty, vibrant sister; an artist-father and safe business-oriented son; Irene and Mireille fantasize whereas the son and grandson see only the common, material world about them.

In *Captain Conan* we pass from the last encounters of wartime to peacetime. The only tension propelling the film is that between the formalities of regular military officers and the impulsive movement of Conan and his band of guerrillas. The brutality of the guerrillas is condoned in the beginning, but after the Armistice, the same men who are capable of risking their lives in guerrilla warfare were supposed to become sedate, obedient soldiers. It does not happen, of course, and the ensuing dilemma is placed before the spectators by means of contrasting scenes of violence and formal military deliberations.

Parallels

Parallels are another way of obtaining this progression by counterpoint. Various kinds of parallels can be found in Tavernier's films. Historical parallels are one kind, as discussed previously as part of his realism. In *The Judge and the Assassin*, the assassin Bouvier compares himself to Joan of Arc, as misunderstood by his society as she was by hers. History within history ripples out to encompass twentieth-century social and political injustices. Just as the magistrates and all the righteous want Bouvier guillotined, they also insist that Dreyfus be treated the same way, with no attempt at comprehension. A society prosecutes the individual murderer, yet practices social murders on a larger scale, underscored by the statistics appearing on screen at the end: "Between 1893 and 1898 Sergeant Joseph Bouvier killed 12 children. During the same period, over 2,500 children under 15 years perished in the mines and the silk factories ...assassinated!"

In *Deathwatch*, the science-fiction theme itself is made present for the viewers by the use of Glasgow's Victorian houses, a real past instead of some fabricated, synthetic set. The eye has been replaced by a transplanted camera, requiring advanced scientific know-how, but no jarring visual invention; on the contrary. So even the sci-fi nature of the film defies spectacle and seems familiar and real. As in his historical films, the timegap forces the viewers to discover experiences that are true of their own time and life though set in a different period in the film. Tavernier's realism is what engages the spectators to participate in the filmic experience rather than merely be onlookers at a show.

Even food provides structural parallels. In *'Round Midnight* Lady Ace (played by Bobby Hutcherson) tries hard to find the ingredients in Paris for jambalaya (southern home cooking) while the Frenchman Francis's mother remains proud of her *quenelles*, a classic Lyonnais dish. When Dale leaves New York at the beginning of the film, we see his friend dying in a hotel room; when the film ends and we hear of

Dale's death, we know it must have been in a hotel room that looked like his friend's. The image itself need not be presented as it is already held in the spectator's mind. Because Dexter Gordon had a daughter, Tavernier had the idea of using daughters for both Dale and Francis. The visit to Francis's family in Lyons brings back familial longings to Dale and propels the return to New York and to his own daughter, a parallel to Francis's daughter.

Generational parallels are numerous in Tavernier's films. Before Beatrice's generation, there was already such a problem of communication between father and son when Beatrice's grandfather left for battle and tells his young son, the future Lord de Cortemare and Beatrice's father, that he cannot accompany him yet, giving the son a dagger and ordering him to watch after his mother. The young son returns home to find his mother in bed with another man whom he instantly kills with the dagger, then isolates himself in the tower to await his father's return, crying "My Lord God, I hate you." Now that the avenging boy is grown and a failure in his own eyes, he is faced with his daughter's purity, which he cannot abide as a judgment upon himself. Conforming with the laws of the power struggle, the only way he can maintain his sense of existence is to defile her. When she approaches his bed at the end of the film, having discovered his desecration or murder of everything dear to her, even her beloved birds, she carries the same dagger he used to kill his mother's lover. François merely points to his heart and says, "Here." As she plunges the dagger, she says: "My Lord God, I hate you."

The Presence of a Look

In *Daddy Nostalgia*, the father, while recovering, plays a debonair role for his daughter to the end. The wife appears to remain aloof and oddly uninvolved in their final joyful moments. Yet as soon as the daughter departs, the father's smile disappears and his real physical pain appears on his face. Then he turns to his wife for support and we realize that she had remained cognizant of his pain and of the performance throughout, and that she knew she would be utterly alone all too soon. Suddenly we feel a great deal of empathy for her that was utterly absent during the daughter's stay, for she, too, put on a magnificent performance so as to not spoil the last moments of the father and daughter together. And if Caroline left, knowing her father's death was imminent, was it not to preserve a memory of him with their last, perhaps only, happy moments together?

Different Points of View

When you are trying to present the problem of communication created by different points of view, "if you do not give a different angle at one point . . . [y]ou begin doing the opposite of what you are trying to do. You begin dictating to the audience a point of view in a film where you are pretending to explore different points of view" (Jacobowitz et al. 1986, 69).

In *The Clockmaker*, Tavernier sets us up for a traditional viewpoint, opening with a group of men—all of the same political opinion—dining in a Lyons *bistrot*. They discuss the stupidity of those who still vote for the conservative side. Right and wrong seem clearly defined for them. Then Descombes learns of his son's crime and he is alone, with no one to understand or help him understand how this could have happened. The film moves from this initial rupture between father and son to the final reconciliation, a reconciliation that would never have occurred had the rupture not happened first (Zarader 1985, 249). As Tavernier himself noted, Descombes takes his son's side not just because Bernard is his son, but because he has changed his moral values, rejecting the clichéd cultural ones of the opening scene—irrespective of political orientation—and adopting those of personal understanding (Benoit 1974, 12).

The police chief Guiboud and Descombes, two fathers concerned about their sons, each one lonely, are brought together on numerous occasions, yet grow further and further apart:

> the impossibility of this relationship is revealed in casual details: for instance, the manifestly blue-blooded dog which [Guiboud played by] Rochefort trails on its walks and delivers to a maid at his daughter's manifestly expensive home while Noiret [playing Descombes] goes home to his flat-above-the-shop. (Milne 1977, 123)

The police chief tries to defend the values of the reigning class that coincide with his social aspirations. Their differences are reflected in the animals themselves amid which the park scene is set. The impala move freely in the natural setting of the zoo while Guiboud keeps a tight leash on the immaculately groomed poodle, giving it orders.

Commentator Bion notes that the story about a little boy, recounted by Michel Descombes to Guiboud, has nothing to do with the subject of the film, "yet the very different reactions of the two men clearly reveal their unique mind sets and the complex bond that is forming between them" (Bion 1984, 18). In the film Guiboud finds the boy's remark insolent, the sign of a bad boy ("He was impudent!" or the French: "C'est du culot!"); Michel finds the open attempt at communication with a stranger to be a sign of friendship ("I didn't think so! He just couldn't help saying it. He was really interested, really loved me," or the French: "Mais non, qui vient tout seul vous dire quelque chose qui l'a étonné et qu'il ne peut pas garder pour lui, enfin. Ah! je crois que personne ne m'a jamais aimé comme ce petit garçon"). The boy had come up to him and said "How you've changed!" What the boy meant is left entirely up to the spectator; what the spectator cannot miss are the totally different interpretations made by the two men. Yet both fathers are concerned about their son's future; both are perplexed when faced with the demands, the revolts of youth (Bion 1984, 25). Because of these different views, we come to accept Michel's interpretation. It appears more human, more understanding, truer, whereas the police chief keeps applying computerized formulas, rejecting comprehension and understanding of another individual. Many of the scenes that show us the different points of view have no causal relationship to the apparent subject of the film, a son's conviction for murder. Juxtaposed with other scenes, however, they are crucial to the spectators' change of opinion, their preference of Michel, their rejection of the politically and socially acceptable argument for murder and passion. The real reason—disgust with the reigning system—is much too damning of the system, but the spectator shares in this disgust by the end of the film.

Use of Dialogue

Different Levels of Meaning

Dialogue often says one thing and means another. Tavernier had noticed this characteristic of David Rayfiel's scripts in *Jeremiah Johnson* and *Three Days of the Condor*, which gave him the desire to write a script with Rayfiel. In the resultant *Deathwatch*, Roddy has denied his beloved but estranged wife any intimacy knowing what she does not, that he has traded his eyes for cameras and that his every action is being watched in a television production studio. Their encounter before his departure in pursuit of Katherine is one of the rare comic scenes in the film. The spectators understand his rejection of his wife's affections; he does not want a love scene between them displayed publicly. The dialogue itself tells a different story, for his wife interprets the rejection as proof he is unloving. The implanted camera thus presents a public view of all the private scenes depicted. The voyeuristic role of any film-goer is satirized by the futuristic premise underlying the film.

In *Life and Nothing But* Irene's husband, who is also Alice's lover, is an unknown soldier of another sort, other than statistically unidentifiable. Neither woman knows of his other existence, nor suspects it. Major Dellaplane discovers the two sides of one individual, but jealousy between the two women, the common motor of comedies, never rears its head. It does, however, bring suspense to the film as the spectator fears the discovery by the women and foresees only heartbreak for both of them, a tragedy instead of a comedy. Tavernier often treads the fine line between the two without ever falling completely into one mode or the other.

Different levels of understanding exist for various dialogues in *A Sunday in the Country*: we feel the character speaking is hiding something, trying to express something other than the words spoken. All of Ladmiral's conversations with his daughter fall into this category. He wants to know if she has a lover, but will not ask, and she will never tell. He wants to say how much he loves her pursuit of adventure; she feels obliged to pay her respects yet is bored beyond belief with the measured bourgeois life of her father and her brother's family.

Dialogue/Silence

When many modern directors were relegating dialogue to the back burner (words only hide reality), Tavernier engaged the two most experienced masters of dialogue in film history, Pierre Bost and Jean Aurenche for *The Clockmaker*. As part of a detective story where interrogation comprises the main objective, the dialogue was all important. Whereas Descombes is very careful to say only what he means, the police commissioner "talks all the time," Tavernier explains, "but without ever saying anything about himself—which is a way of hiding behind words" (Braucourt 1974, 62). All the action leads up to the trial; Tavernier's mastery is such that no time is lost on the tedious arguments of the lawyers. Only five shots are needed to dispense with the legal formality condemning the son to twenty years in prison (Benoit 1974, 7). Tavernier uses dialogue and silence to communicate emotion, not to propel the plot. The numerous silences communicate the acute sense of waiting and anguish.

The juxtaposition of differing languages accentuates the theme of incommunicability, estrangement, and silence. In *Daddy Nostalgia*, the mother is French and the father English and both are bilingual. Early on, the father says to his wife in English: "You never speak to me in English anymore." Only twice does the mother speak English to her husband. The first time, the father has been recalling their happy wartime memories and sings part of the film's title song, "These Foolish Things," to her. She comments in English: "That was a long time ago. Go to bed, Tony, go to bed," as she goes upstairs. He mutters "You used to say, 'Come to bed,'" underscoring the change time has wrought. Here, too, even in the language, past and present are juxtaposed to communicate to the spectator a direct feeling of a relationship. Later, when they are sitting alone in the garden, "Any news?" He replies in French, "*Pardon, chérie*?" not comprehending. No explanation, Hollywood style, is ever given.

Off-Screen Events and Cultural Artifacts

Events that occur off-screen are often used to engage spectators. Irene's love story in *A Sunday in the Country* intrigues us, but is never revealed to us. Off-stage executions and rapes in *The Judge and the Assassin* have the same effect.

In *A Sunday in the Country*, the spectator cannot help but find references to other works that exist outside the film being watched. The film clearly references Impressionism, especially Monet's gardens and his discovery of purple as the color of shadows: the father says he would like to do a portrait of his son, he would be purple—his own shadow, of course. Tavernier wanted to capture the light and mood of Impressionism, which itself, was an art in transition, the destruction of the classical principles of form and organization, and, at the same time, an exploration of the possibilities of light and color, the complexities of a scene: "I wanted it to be close to an Impressionist painting, to

Figure 8: Cafe-dansant.   *A Sunday in the Country*

have a great depth of field with colors but no filters or reflectors"
(Yakir 1984, 22). Renoir's café-by-the-river cannot help but come to
mind when the daughter accompanies her father there for a last dance
(figure 8).

In *A Week's Vacation*, at a dinner party during Laurence's crisis,
Tavernier has Noiret appear in just one moving scene as the character
he played a decade before in *The Clockmaker*, talking about his son in
prison. The crises reflect one another if the spectator is familiar with
the earlier film as a cultural artifact. This technique, which he will
repeat, engages the spectator in making use of his other cinematic
experiences when interpreting the film, just as he does in real life. The
same technique is used in *Captain Conan* where the Bouvier of *The
Judge and the Assassin* reappears as the cook for the commander in
charge. He is gleefully skinning a wild boar just shot by Conan.
Coming in the latter part of the film, the echo underscores Conan's
dependency on murder as a way of life. Will Conan turn into another
Bouvier after the war? Fortunately for society, Conan will die too soon
afterwards to commit Bouvier's post-war brutalities.

Butterfly Effect

Events end up appearing linked thanks to a Butterfly Effect, whereby
an apparently insignificant comment or event results in major
consequences, as explained by chaos theory. When Cordier is teaching
Rose to shoot a gun, she says, "You've got an idea in your head," and
he denies it, saying, "I do things without thinking. Later I understand."
After she ends up shooting Nono and Huguette, it looks like he trained
her to shoot for that purpose. Yet the events cannot be considered
causal in the traditional sense of plot development. He could not have
known that they would try to rough her up and she would manage to
shoot them in self-defense. There is no willed intent to cause her to kill
them; in fact, he even invites her to go away with him for the day and
go fishing when he knows his wife is going to be on the rampage. Her
choice is to decline the offer. Contrast this with *Les Liaisons
dangereuses* where the plot consists of Madame de Merteuil's conscious
and stated desire to have Cécile seduced so Count Gercourt will not
marry the virgin he has publicly advertised he would. Even though her
plot fails, her intended cause and effect are what drive events. In *Clean
Slate*, Cordier cannot know when he shoots the pimps that his Chief
will show up and can be convinced to go to the brothel where he will
brag so much about having disposed of the pimps that he will appear
the logical culprit. Discovering the suspected cause afterwards
generates a feeling of horror in the spectator, a respect for the
unpredictability of events.

Breaching the Hierarchical System, the Frozen Form

All of the above techniques used to destroy traditional plot progression
are geared to breaching the frozen forms of the hierarchical power
structure. In fracturing it, they satirize its inherently sado-masochistic
nature. Breaching the closed walls of the structure is often the main
theme—one might even call it the plot—of a Tavernier film; it is always
present in the background. As mentioned in the preface to this book,
Americans in general tend to think well of power: they want it, they
respect it, even though they may intellectually acknowledge that its use,
as with the atomic bomb, can be too destructive. This last discovery
about power is only fifty years old in our culture and we were the
country exercising the power, not the object of its application. No

living Americans have memories of another country physically invading their homeland—unless they came to America for asylum from such an invasion. All Frenchmen born before World War II have such memories. They have a different emotional experience of power than Americans do. So it is hardly surprising that American critics generally failed to comprehend *Clean Slate* at all.[1] Only David Ansen of *Newsweek* understood that the film was part of an ongoing examination by Tavernier of the relationship of victim and victimizer (Ansen 1983, 53). The horror discovered when experiencing this film is that of the *roman noir* or thriller. The Marquis de Sade's *120 Days of Sodom* may well be the first modern example of the genre. At any rate, a knowledge of his philosophy helps understand *Clean Slate* and *Beatrice* in particular as well as Tavernier's continual thrusts at the power structure and its system of thought elsewhere.

Notes

1. The critic of *Commonweal*, for instance, recounts the Nigerians' explanation for an Englishman driving into the harbor one night after coming out of his usual pub: he had gone "wawa." "Wawa" is British slang, an acronym for "West Africa Wins Again." It was universally acknowledged that going "wawa" was not always self-destructive. It could be a way to survive as well as perish, a saving accommodation one made to the climate, the conditions and the inevitable depression Europeans feel when stuck in some colonial backwater. The critic concludes that "judging from . . . *Coup de Torchon*, this form of mental illness was equally widespread in French West Africa" (Westerbeck 1983, 86-87).

4

Sado-Masochism, the Power Structure, and Causal Plot

Definition

Freud wrote,

> With the pair of opposites sadism-masochism, the process may be
> represented as follows:
> (a) Sadism consists in acts of violence, or power upon some other
> person as its object;

In *Beatrice*, for example, the father first forces Beatrice to submit
against her will to his desires. In *Clean Slate* it is found when the
pimps cause Cordier to fall down backwards in front of his servant or
when his chief literally boots him out his office door.

> (b) This object is abandoned and replaced by the subject's self.
> Together with the turning round upon the self, the change from an
> active to a passive aim in the instinct is also brought about.

The father forces his daughter, Beatrice, to revolt against him, making
himself the object of her hatred. Cordier, pushed to the limit by the
pimps, seems forced to shoot them to terminate the annoyance they are
causing him and others.

> (c) Again another person is sought as object; this person, in
> consequence of the alteration which has taken place in the aim of the
> instinct, has to take over the original role of the subject.

Beatrice is now the subject in the father's sado-masochistic experience in self-realization. Cordier becomes the executioner.

> Case (c) is the condition commonly termed masochism. Satisfaction follows in this case by way of the original sadism in that the passive ego placing itself in phantasy back in its former situration, which, however, has now been given up to another subject outside the self. Whether there is, besides this, a more direct masochistic satisfaction is highly doubtful. A primary masochism not derived in the manner I have described from sadism, does not appear to be met with (Freud 1915, 416)

The Witness—the Other's Look

In order for the sadistic act to be self-defining, it must be known, seen by others, and not merely by the recipient, the object. The sadist needs a public to feel the realization of his or her existence, the confirmation of identity (Damisch 1967, 51). As a consequence, eroticism, not voluptuousness, characterizes the passionate encounters. Because the sexual act is important only as a sign of one's existence, the sado-masochist never loses his awareness of his act. There is never any abandonment of oneself, no voluptuousness in the sexual act. The only way the sadist can join the other partner is by means of spectacle. The performance, in the stage sense, is essential to the enjoyment, to the satisfaction that the sadist needs in order to feel himself exist.

Sitting at the dining table, the police chief Cordier manages to lord it over Nono, especially when his mistress Rose is present. As a witness Rose laughs with him at Nono's stupidity and at Huguette's cuckoldry. The spectators too are made witnesses, for we are the only ones to gloat with Cordier at Nono being slapped by Huguette when he complains that the coffee is salty; we are the only ones who saw Cordier dump the salt-shaker into his coffee when Nono momentarily absented himself from the table.

The Sadist in *Clean Slate*

When the local pimp humiliates Cordier, he has a companion with him to watch; when Cordier's superior boots him out the door, he, too, has onlookers present, within his office and outside in the reception room. Cordier's wife intensifies her badgering of him when Nono (her brother-lover) or Rose is present. Indeed, it might be argued that she would not be interested in Nono at all if she were not performing with him continually under the nose of Cordier. On the other hand, when Cordier kills, or arranges to have others killed, he takes great care that there are no witnesses. It is never his fault if there are—and those he necessarily gets rid of as well. Thus it is that he must kill the African servant Friday when Rose says, in Friday's presence, that Cordier killed her husband. In order to maintain his independence and not be caught in a subject-object relationship, Cordier must get rid of the witness, Friday, or become the object of his look, knowing that Friday knows he is the murderer.

The Sociopolitical Consequences of Freedom from the Power Structure

Sade's philosophy leads essentially to anarchy, refusing the social pact which, according to Sade, protects the weak and threatens the strong. The strong know very well how to use the law to their advantage, but the law, in that case, remains superior to them. The law is always the ultimate master. The passions of a neighbor are infinitely less to be feared than the injustice of the law (Sade had spent thirty years in prison thanks to a *lettre de cachet* for having given a few pills to prostitutes who subsequently suffered serious gas pains from them). The passions of the neighbor are restrained by one's own, whereas nothing stops the injustices of the law, because nothing is above the law. Therefore, even if the law serves man on occasion, it also oppresses him by limiting his self-realization. This explains why Sade was at home during the revolutionary period; it represented a period without laws (Blanchot 1965, 610-11). Tavernier has repeatedly selected historical moments of transition when those in power (the Subjects) are about to be overthrown and society has a momentary chance of developing a new system and of freeing itself from the old laws.

The Totally Free Being

Complete liberty requires that one be capable of doing anything. By making the greatest destruction and the greatest affirmation coincide, one has proven oneself to be free. The liberty to be oneself depends solely on the power one has to dominate others without becoming the object of their look.[1] Were one to become the object of the other, one would thereby lose the freedom so sought. This explains why Cordier does not yield to his attraction for the schoolteacher, for he fears the emotional attachment that would result from it and bind him to her, to her look. He would therein lose his ability to act freely.

Juliette, La Durand: Examples from Sade

In *Justine*, Saint-Fond proposes a plan to ruin two-thirds of France by famine. Juliette hesitates and is immediately threatened: hunger and death are superior to her. La Durand poisons without qualms; when the government of Venice asks her to spread the plague, however, she becomes fearful for her own life and is immediately condemned. Death is her master. Cordier does not appear as weak as Sade's greatest heroines. The ending of the film leaves the spectator wondering if he might not just be capable of killing everyone else and even himself. The sense of his complete freedom from any kind of law or restraint is what is so disquieting. Though neither Sade nor Tavernier is proposing such a free-wheeling society, both use its potential reality to question the hierarchical power structure in place.

Escaping the Subject-Object Bond

In *Clean Slate*, all the local White entrepreneurs treat Cordier as an object to be manipulated. Yet he refuses to enter into the subject-object bond. He cannot bear to arrest a criminal, which would amount to treating him or her as object. When he begins killings, it is never as a subject using the object to react to him and thereby provide proof of his identity. The initial sequence of frames is highly significant: he provides a fire to warm the starving African boys during the eclipse of the sun, but runs away as soon as it is lit so that they will not have to defer to his White presence and feel subservient in order to warm themselves. The only person who does not engage him in the subject-object bond is the schoolteacher to whom Cordier seems to confide his true feelings. Were he to enter into a sexual relationship with her, would his freedom be threatened? This is one of the unanswered dilemmas posed by the film.

Resultant Alienation

As the only relationship understood and practiced by the other inhabitants of his village is that of subject-object, Cordier's acts to rid the world of those who treat others as slaves (objects) must remain anonymous or the others would put a stop to them, taking charge as subjects for fear of becoming Cordier's next object. This anonymity reinforces his isolation. It permits him to remain free, above the law, in Sadian terms, but alone.

Techniques

Filmic Tension—Spectator or Witness

Unless placed in the context of Sade's exploration of the hierarchical power structure, Bertrand Tavernier's *Clean Slate* confounds the spectator by its profound originality. It forces the spectator to change opinions and feelings three times regarding the main protagonist, the police chief Cordier (played by Philippe Noiret).

In most films by other directors, we come to know the protagonist better; we understand or like him or her better, or the reverse. The development of our feelings is a linear progression of some sort, a one-way street. Exceptionally, there are films such as Hitchcock's *Psycho*, in which we develop a sympathy for a bad individual based on the withholding of a truth we only discover later. The ending may disappoint us, but then we can usually blame society or destiny and not the protagonist. *Clean Slate* does none of that. The film can be divided into three parts, each defined by the reaction the spectator has to Cordier.

In the first third, approximately, Cordier appears somewhat revolting and despicable, so we do not approve of him. He is not dressed neatly like the other White residents of Bourkassa. He is a "slob" (figure 9). In the middle part, when he starts secretly killing off the town's *salauds* such as the pimps, we would like to have a friend like that to get rid of all the *salauds* with whom we have to deal to get things accomplished. Sartre defined *salauds* (bastards) to be those who consider themselves essential to the world and order others about to prove it. And in the last part, we are appalled when Cordier kills Friday, the Black African who was witness to Rose's accusation. We

Figure 9: First Impression. *Clean Slate*

Figure 10: A Pushover. *Clean Slate*

Figure 11: Deleting Pimps. *Clean Slate*

Figure 12: Nail him! *Clean Slate*

become even fearful of him, for Friday appeared totally harmless.

If placed in the Sadian context, we can begin to grasp why Tavernier has done this, for it fully implicates the spectator's own participation in the sado-masochistic / subject-object bonding. First we see Cordier being treated as an object by not very reputable characters in the presence of witnesses. Our Western cultural heritage has taught us that a real man does not permit himself to be publicly pushed down by pimps without a fight (figure 10); in the twelfth century a duel would have been mandatory. Cordier puts up no fight whatsoever; he appears as a lamentable representation of the human species. The pimps push him around and knock him down; his wife cuckolds him flagrantly in his own house; he does not even protect his mistress Rose from public beatings by her husband. When he goes to see his superior, he is physically booted out the door to more witnesses, not once, but twice. He appears to be a dilapidated example of mankind.

Then Tavernier flips the coin on us. In the next series of encounters there are no witnesses—except the spectator. We discover our man Cordier has set up appearances so that no one would believe him capable of actually committing the acts he does. He shoots the pimps (figure 11), and sets up his superior to take the blame. Then the priest, pounding nails into Christ on the cross, counsels Cordier to get rid of Marcaillou (figure 12). So he shoots his mistress' rotten husband Marcaillou, though not particularly because he is a bad husband; rather because he beats on anyone he can, native Africans as well as his wife (figure 13). By sawing the floorboards in half in the middle of the night, he causes the town slumlord to fall into the hole of the public latrines he owns, thereby getting them removed. He catches his wife's lover/supposed brother Nono peeping at the schoolteacher taking a shower; this gives Cordier an excuse to beat the hell out of him, a beating Nono can hardly complain about to Cordier's wife, his mistress, since he cannot tell her it was because he was watching the schoolteacher take a shower. Cordier has the same attraction as Vautrin does in Balzac. He has seduced us with our dream of the exercise of power over others without suffering reprisals. Suddenly he has earned our respect and admiration.

Now Tavernier flips the coin on us again, for the next person Cordier shoots is Friday, a Black servant who has done nothing bad except return the body of Rose's husband to her door for burial. In her exasperation at having to deal with her bastard of a husband even after his death, Rose blurts out in Friday's presence the fact that Cordier

Figure 13: Deleting Marcaillou.   *Clean Slate*

shot her husband. Now Friday has become a witness, a witness to an act that had no witness, except the spectator. Herein comes our discomfort. If being a witness is sufficient cause for being murdered, then our admirable Cordier might just turn on us next. Maybe he was not such a desirable buddy to have after all? Or is the spectator the guilty one? Thus our malaise during the remainder of the film when he sets up the other *salauds* to get their just desserts. Prior to Friday's murder we might have been delighted to see Rose shoot Nono and Cordier's wife; and we cannot blame Cordier for getting rid of a little tramp like Rose either. But we have become uncomfortable witnesses.

To understand a Tavernier film is to understand a problem Tavernier is exploring. In *Clean Slate*, the search for freedom from the subject-object social bond constitutes the basis of the inquiry. The plot avoids the problem of the French Revolution wherein the revolutionaries merely replaced the aristocrats as new masters with their newfound power over others. Here, Cordier never accedes to the public position of power, for there are no witnesses to his strength-proving acts. No one believes him capable of action warranting esteem—except the schoolteacher, the only one functioning outside the subject-object power structure: she does not judge anyone, but merely seeks to understand.

In the sado-masochistic relationship, the subject's sense of identity is magnified considerably when a witness is present to validate the object's response to the subject. The witness, however, in being witness, enters into the subject-object bond by virtue of the power he has now acquired over the others, the former subject and object. In fact, he is now the real subject, the persons observed having become the object of his observation. The witness is no more free of the bond than the original subject-object participants. Thus Tavernier exposes the error indulged in by the spectator when he revels in the stealthy destruction of the town's *salauds*. Our flippant belief that we would all be free if we could just eliminate all those trying to exercise their power over us has just been dashed. As any participation in the subject-object structure precludes freedom, Tavernier has caught the spectators in one of their secret delusions and made them uncomfortable with their role in this structure, even as witness only. If one could escape the power of others by quietly eliminating them, how could the individual achieve self-realization? Does such a freedom lead only to isolation and solitude? Tavernier does not attempt to answer; his work is always an exploration of the problem. Here he pulls away the veils concealing the spectators' subconscious participation in the structure.

Reinforcing Film Techniques—Above and Below Camera Shots

In the scene where Cordier visits his superior and asks what to do about the humiliating pimps, Cordier receives the easy answer: hit back twice as hard. The superior makes his point by physically booting Cordier out of his office twice. In the first shot, the camera, inside the office, assumes the point of view of the superior (figure 14). It looks down on Cordier lying in the outer office and is superior to him. In the next sequence, when Cordier is thrown out of the office the second time, the camera placed on the floor of the outer office assumes Cordier's point of view (figure 15). In a tilted frame, the camera and Cordier look up at the aggressor and humiliator and find themselves in an inferior position. The effect of this sequence is to establish a hierarchy of meaning: Cordier, the nearest and lowest (read inferior) figure; the police chief, the distant, higher (read superior) figure.[2] The camera angle contributes enormously to the spectators' impression that Cordier is not manly.

Because Europeans have so often physically experienced the

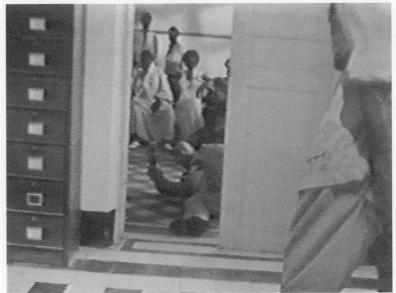

Figure 14: Shot from above. *Clean Slate*

Figure 15: Shot from below. *Clean Slate*

destructive effects of the power structure, their most serious interest lies in dismantling that structure and therein permitting the exploration of other relationships that do not have its ultimately destructive consequences. The traditional narrative forms based on causal development have always supported the power structure, leading to the triumph of good (or stronger, more cunning, better connected), the downfall of evil (or ignorance, sloth, and especially passions), but never to comprehension of the nature of the structure itself. By generating new forms of storytelling, Tavernier contributes a visual example of how comprehension can replace judgment. Summarizing the plot of *Clean Slate* could only amount to enumerating a series of scenes; there is no causal development to follow. Though there are some losers, no one has won at the end of the film. Cordier is too lonely to be deemed the winner. All of Tavernier's historical works focus on this power structure, undermining it by destroying causal plot development. There are no heroes.

Beatrice[3]

By virtue of the crudity of medieval life and customs, *Beatrice* is a stark caricature of today's hierarchical power structure. There is but one conflict. As the spectators are told in a preparatory announcement, the action is guided strictly by *pulsions intérieures*, or the characters' emotions. There are those like François de Cortemare who can define their identity only within the sado-masochistic power structure, and those like Beatrice who seek only to love, demanding nothing more in return.

As a ten-year-old child, the future Lord de Cortemare is deserted by his father, who refuses to let him accompany him to battle. Presented with a dagger as a parting gift from his father, he is instructed to defend his mother. He obeys. Returning to the castle, he runs to show his mother the dagger he has received only to discover his mother in bed with her lover. Instantly he stabs the lover, immediately discovering power. He orders her to make the body disappear, announcing to her, "My father is not avenged for you never betrayed him." Having been witness to the scene, he now retains the power over her of the secret between them. Only the return of his father might have taught him love, but three months later he learns of his father's death. He has no one to turn to for love, for sharing emotions. He is forced to reign, to be the master, alone.

He in turn goes to war, but takes his son with him and does not return for four years. During that time, Beatrice discovers the greed and avarice of others, becoming the object of their cunning. She is forced to sell to another landowner. The notary disparages her lands as useless, left uncultivated by the serfs. To obtain the sum she needs, she must even sell a tapestry and other family belongings. Defenseless in a man's world, she gets no support from her grandmother. She desperately desires the return of her father in hopes of his love, but also protection. She is alone.

Having received word that he will return during a full moon, great preparations are made in anticipation. His mother gloats before the servants over what a poor repast he will find if he does not show during the full moon as announced. It may be her last chance to express her own existence before witnesses. "He'll be served raw hedgehog with all its quills and may he choke on it!" Beatrice, knowing nothing of the murder of the lover by her father, replies: "Cannot you hate in silence?" As she has no interest in power as self-defining, she does not understand, even intuitively, her grandmother's need for witnesses.

But he does not return for seven moons. And when he and his comrades are spotted from afar, there is no time to catch hedgehogs, so an appropriate dinner is prepared, though not the glorious one he would have had six months earlier. When he first lays eyes on Beatrice, who has blossomed into a full-grown woman in the four years he has been gone, he says not a word to her, instinctively turning away to give attention to his new female possession picked up on the road home. It is a sadist's blatant way of imposing authority on someone esteemed enough to be worth hurting. There is no sharing of affection as there is between Beatrice and her brother Arnaud. Seeing that affection makes him want all the more to punish Beatrice. It is the only way he can relate to people.

As his daughter prefers that Arnaud recount their exploits rather than hear them from the strangers who accompanied her father, de Cortemare immediately begins to recount them himself, having previously refused to do so at the behest of the old man present. But he does so only to admit he killed no Englishmen, only his own men. Then he proceeds to defile his son before all, accusing him of being a coward because "in battle his bowels leak out beneath him in a pool of stinking excrement" and he himself had to turn back to save Arnaud before he "changed into a pillar of shit." There were no heroic exploits to recount. And having finished dining, he turns to see his son still eating. He shoves his face in his plate; then, pulling it up for all to see, announces, "When your father has done, you're done!" Thus he publicly affirms his authority, his identity as ruler of the household, but does so only by hurting and defiling those about him.

After satisfying his lust on the sick woman he picked up on the road, he retreats to the solitude of the tower, but Beatrice follows and confronts him with his own unhappiness. Touched by her attentions, he plays a chess game with her. Seeing that she is about to checkmate his king, she makes an alternative move. He calls her on it and has her take back the rook and make the move that would defeat him, saying she was permitted to beat him that night. Then he hears his son howling in fear from nightmares. Later, he overhears Beatrice comforting him with tenderness he himself has never known. As he despises his son as the reflection of his weak side, he cannot bear Arnaud receiving the love he cannot receive. So the following morning he has Beatrice summoned to come bathe him, though he has plenty of servants to do so. And while she bathes him, he reprimands her for what she sold to obtain his release.

Other characters besides Beatrice are caring and sharing, such as her own brother, Arnaud—but he appears to have so little consequence. And the half-witted four- or five-year-old child, Jehan, who reacts instinctively with caresses to soothe pain, cries when he witnesses cruelty, and trembles when he feels impending disaster, having no ability to express his emotions other than physically. These characters act as counterpoints to the sado-masochistic impulses of the others.

Hearing noises at night, Beatrice descends to discover her father and company returning with the spoils of a raid. He tries to force his son to possess Nicolette, one of the castle wenches. Catching his daughter watching, he obliges her to give her clothes to Nicolette. When his mother tries to intervene, he yanks the jewels from around her neck and gives them to Nicolette to further defile both his mother and his daughter, thereby proving his power before witnesses.

Later Beatrice finds him writhing and howling from the loathing he feels for himself. Then he enters the women's bedroom. He makes the sign of the cross backward standing before the statue of the Virgin. He orders Beatrice to come kneel before the Virgin; upon her refusal (she is still huddled in bed), he pulls her out and forces her to ask forgiveness for the sin she is about to commit. He proceeds to rape her, relishing in the fact, before the other women, that she is now a whore. Her resistance only adds to his glory.

He awaits her every revolt to feel himself exist. Claiming to love him in exchange for his amethyst ring, she secretly visits a sorcerer with a puppet she has sewn in his image to have a spell cast on him. Unfortunately she is followed by her father, who can only find satisfaction in her acts against him. When she tries to tell the family priest of her father's violation of God's will, he pleads "little power" and counsels, "a woman must submit to her father and husband as she did to God" because "one of a lower station in life cannot judge someone higher." He, too, supports the power structure until Cortemare asks the priest to marry him to his daughter. The priest knows then that the daughter has not lied and threatens to go to the bishop to have him excommunicated, using a power of another sort.

François de Cortemare does not fear hell, however, because he is already living it, his soul tortured by the sadistic acts he has committed. But saved from a burning hut into which he has thrown himself to end his torture, he cannot resist an even greater outrage. For the sadist requires ever greater proof of his destructive powers to feel himself exist. He leads Beatrice and Lemartin, the seigneur who had bought his lands, to believe they will be wed. Seeing both of them sharing a tender love for each other, he cannot resist smashing their hopes of happiness. He tells her afterwards how he informed Lemartin that he had already possessed his daughter, but would sew her up if it pleased him. Thus he revenges himself on the man who took his lands from him and simultaneously leaves his daughter without any hope of escape. As he witnesses her despair, his joy increases and he embellishes even more on the story he told Lemartin.

Pregnant, Beatrice begs Arnaud to kick her in the belly to cause her to abort. Unfortunately Cortemare arrives while this is happening. Knowing he can get an even greater reaction from Beatrice by punishing Arnaud, he condemns him to be the prey in the next day's hunt, dressed as a girl. Beatrice and the castle wenches are all forced to join the hunt so as to witness his dishonor. When caught, Cortemare orders the wenches to indulge in his son's body; Beatrice rides away, too sickened by her father's cruelty to continue to witness it.

Stopping by a stream to wash the tears from her face, she discovers the half-wit Jehan who simply ran away when the horrors became too great. He has done his own penance for wishing evil thoughts, but now, upon seeing Beatrice, he runs from her. She is no

longer pure enough for him. On her way through the village, she finds
the sorceress-saint burning at the stake, the populace eagerly watching.
She again leaves in disgust. When she enters her chamber, she finds
her beloved magpies butchered, with the same dagger François had
used to kill his mother's lover. She proceeds to her father's bed where
he awaits her, carrying both the birds and the dagger. Knowing he has
pushed her to the limit, he now makes her the subject, showing her
where to strike his heart with the dagger. She drives the dagger home,
then caresses the face of the Virgin with her blood-stained hands. There
the film ends.

We, the witnesses to the murder, can only approve of her. She had
no other escape from such a father. At the same time, we pity him, for
he has been suffering from abandonment since he was ten years old.
Cortemare did every sadistic thing imaginable to force her to become
the subject who would treat him as an object. The full sado-masochistic
cycle has been materialized. The self-destructive nature of the
hierarchical power structure lies exposed.

There was no plot in the sense of causal development of events,
yet there was plenty of action. The action, however, was all a
consequence of emotions and most of the emotions themselves born of
the power structure.

The Judge and the Assassin

In 1893 Bouvier (Jacques Vacher in reality) began a five-year stint of
sadistic rapes of thirteen-year-old youths, starting in Lourdes. The
resultant self-hatred is evident as soon as the credits are over: he is
pointing a gun down his throat, though we have no idea why. But like
François de Cortemare, he needs witnesses for his demise, the more the
better. At that moment there are none. After the war, he flees to see
Louise, whom he knows, or should have known, will reject him, just
as Cortemare knows he will be rejected by Beatrice. His masochistic
pleasure is guaranteed by the choice of his object. She is sure to revolt
and treat him as an object, just as he treated those he raped and
murdered. When she refuses once again his gifts and offer of marriage,
he grabs her violently and she escapes only by running into the church
sanctuary. Infuriated, he kicks a dog beside the beggar at the church
steps to further inflict pain somewhere and obtain a reaction from by-
standers.

After their church encounter, he goes to her home and waits.

When she does not come, he insults her further by asking her mother for her sixteen-year-old sister instead. He begs a bed for the night in the stable, stating he does not want to be alone. Alone, he would be faced with his own void. He needs witnesses to exist. The mother of course refuses to accord him the company of the sister who is terrified. Knowing of no other way to inflict pain on Louise, to reach her, he goes to her workplace and asks for the return of his letters and photo, guaranteeing an encounter and a final rejection. Upon receiving it, he shoots her and then himself. The bullets, however, are not terminal for either of them and he recovers to some extent. When no one is paying his bill any longer, he is discharged from the hospital into society.

Seeking refuge, he goes to the seminary where he studied for two years before going into the army. He asks to take care of the organ, to be the servant, but the priest wants nothing to do with him, whereupon he accuses the priesthood of having raped him while he was under their care.

When we first meet the judge on his case, he is in the company of a magistrate who was forced to resign his post and leave French Indochina. The latter has been reading "their" enemy, Mirabeau, who says of murder that "we are all potential murderers, but we find legal outlets for our need to kill; industry, colonial trade, war, anti-Semitism." He has chosen anti-Semitism because "it is not dangerous, it is fashionable, and has the Church's blessing." The prejudices of the conservative powerhouse are clearly outlined. Villedieu will be Judge Rousseau's principal witness, his esteem of the judge's persecution of Bouvier justifying the judge's existence.

After locating Bouvier and obtaining a confession from him, Judge Rousseau writes an editorial for the newspaper in which he claims "the law must come down hard with heavier prison terms for hobos. Parasites who seek only to satisfy their hunger and sexual appetite. This year I counted 18,067 offenses committed by these asocial persons." Mirabeau seems to have left the magistrature out of his list of outlets for murder. The judge's own glory (he seeks the medal of the Legion of Honor) depends on obtaining capital punishment for the rapist, not a plea of insanity. The possibility that the 18,067 offenses may have been the consequences of society's injustices is never entertained.

Bouvier, seeking a judgment of insanity, writes a letter to the doctors examining him, noting that if anyone was to be held responsible for his crimes, it should be "the doctor who released [him]" from the Dole asylum to which he had been committed after attempting suicide following the shooting of Louise. But the doctors are not likely to impugn one of their own as the individual responsible for Bouvier's numerous rapes and murders. That verdict would condemn the power system. Furthermore, as the ex-magistrate Villedieu assures the judge, Bouvier is poor, so there is no chance of an insane verdict from the medical profession. He observes further, "if there were war, Bouvier would make a good soldier and serve his country well." When there is no war, society makes war on vagabonds.

The judge's propensity to murder is further underscored after Bouvier has attempted to stab him in the prison cell. The judge goes directly to Rose and proceeds to sodomize her over the kitchen table. Then he becomes ashamed of himself and cries in her skirts: "I think I need you." To make amends, he even insists on introducing her to his mother, which turns out to be a way of defiling her more. His mother does not even deign to address her, speaking to the judge only of Bouvier's attempt to stab him. In revolt after Bouvier's execution, Rose not only leaves the judge, but rejoins her factory workers in a political demonstration.

Bouvier's final letter to Louise says, "You know, Louise, if the Judge isn't genuine, it's because he does not know the poor. . . . He didn't come from a family of twelve where you fight hunger to stay alive." Whereas Bouvier pleas for understanding of the social circumstances that formed the individual, the judge judges according to predetermined values. We learn, however, that if the doctors would not impugn one of their own profession, they do not appreciate being led to kill a lunatic.

The ending that shows revolt against oppression is too polemical and is, perhaps, Tavernier's weakest ending. Leaving the viewers with their disgust for the judge would have left them facing their own prejudices. By presenting socialism as an answer, he allows the viewers to turn their disgust against other hierarchical power structures, such as workers' unions with their no less corrupt and self-serving magnates. The spectators can escape from their own prejudices. The film is weakened by falling into the causal plot: because the legal system committed an injustice, there was a workers' uprising. By espousing storytelling, Tavernier weakens his attempt to fracture the frozen social form, the hierarchical power structure.

Life and Nothing But

The hierarchical power structure is satirized on two levels that play in counterpoint. On the one hand, the officials are supposed to locate six bodies of unknown soldiers so the powers that be can perform a ceremony selecting one body to honor the 1.4 million that died in battle. Major Dellaplane's diligence in trying to identify every single body so as to find the missing-in-action underscores the cavalier attitude of the power structure more interested in personal recognition via public ceremony than it is in the dead and their families. That constitutes the official and public levels of satire. On the individual level, we have Irene de Courtil, the daughter-in-law of a senator who expects exceptional services as such and demands them from Major Dellaplane; she is searching for her missing husband. Major Dellaplane, who knows the senator was a collaborator, declares he will give her exactly 1/350,000 of his attention, the same he is giving to the other 350,000 missing in action. And we meet many of the ordinary individuals seeking their loved ones too. The context places the hierarchical power structure in its most ludicrous light.

A Sunday in the Country

M. Ladmiral and Mercedes, his aging housekeeper, depend very much on getting a reaction from each other to maintain a sense of identity. They indulge in the socially acceptable forms of sado-masochism: if one of them is singing, the other sings a different tune louder. Mercedes gets particular pleasure from securing M. Ladmiral's silence in this manner. They delight in contradicting each other. The voice-over tells us "she nurtured his false fear of her leaving him, just to torture him, to feel her control."

M. Ladmiral fears he never painted anything very original because he followed the principles he was taught by his masters, whereas the great impressionist painters such as Monet and Caillebotte adventured into new worlds whose principles were not yet defined. He knows he is caught in the system and that his son is just like him. Seeing his conformity reflected in his son, he criticizes his son for almost everything he does and contradicts him continually. If the father prefers his daughter because she flaunts custom and does as she pleases, as neither he nor his son dare do, he also agrees with everything she says, hoping thereby to gain more of her love and approval. The son, Gonzague, corrects all her errors in a desperate attempt to get his father's attention. Feeling guilty because she spends almost no time with her father, she attempts to belittle her brother in the presence of her father, affirming her superiority in spite of her meager parental care. The daughter Irene is the only one who lives on the edge, flaunting the frozen social forms. The only painting of her father's that she will not sell contains an acrobat; it contains emotion and life. In the meantime, the grandchildren imitate their elders. To feel themselves exist, the boys vie with one another to see who can get the biggest reaction from their parents. One dares throw dirt at the house windows where their parents and grandfather are calmly chatting. Later they dissect and then try to burn an insect, one outdoing the other in cruelty to obtain the admiration of the other. Thus Tavernier exposes the daily and routine family use of sado-masochism and its perpetuation.

Daddy Nostalgia

Caroline makes her father pay dearly for his neglect in her childhood. Knowing his death is pending, and hearing him reminisce about the good old times as better than the present, she blurts, "I do not give a damn about your beautiful great life. It was a beautiful selfish life." He is obviously hurt immensely, but attempts to smooth things over.

Caroline is no less cruel to her mother who, a practicing Catholic, obviously disapproves of Caroline leaving her son and husband, continually criticizing her career as a writer. She has told Caro how "irresponsible" she is, though she is the daughter who comes to care for them at a moment's phone call, her sister having fled to Canada long ago. When Caro expresses some of her nonconventional ideas, her mother says she gave birth to a duck. Caro knows she will soon have to take care of her mother, and one morning when her mother is carefully touching up her lipstick after breakfast, Caro gets on her for not having her eyes operated on, adding bluntly, "I do not want to end up with a blind mother. Your last trip to Paris, you hung on to me like a life-buoy wherever we went." The mother is profoundly hurt, but conceals it until Caro has left the room. When Caro asks if she would come with her and Daddy to Cannes, she makes up an excuse to stay home, feeling most unwanted, yet not wanting to incur more injury by complaining. Again, the sado-masochism perpetuated within the family is exposed even on the deathbed of a beloved.

The Clockmaker

This film posits a revolt against "the same ones coming out on top." The police commissioner Guiboud loses touch with the clock-maker precisely because he clings harder and harder to acceptable forms. As he tells Michel when they are riding together in the train, this case interests him because the son Bernard "represents a lot of others" and wonders, "What have we done to these kids?" The social conventions he embodies prevent him from seeing the prison bars those same conventions represent for youth.

Bernard's attorney also wants to fit the crime into the system. Social and political reasons for the murder of a factory security guard do not interest him, undoubtedly because they condemn the system he sustains. Passions have always been outside the hierarchical power structure. Seventeenth-century classical values mandated that passions be made subservient to honor, the latter being a social value, passions being merely personal. By making the murder a matter of passion, it remains personal. There would be no implied judgment against the sociopolitical system.

Finally rejecting the police commissioner's attempts at friendship by tossing him a tip in the café, Michel proceeds to the church to watch the very complex clock where all the parts must work together in order for it to function properly. Nothing in society seems to be functioning from Michel's point of view. Too many of the individual components have worn out.

Deathwatch

The very premise of *Deathwatch* links sado-masochism and the power structure. The television producer hopes to acquire even greater fame by killing a best-selling writer. In his television series, the viewers both within the film and those watching it become the witnesses. His fame and power is intricately connected to his desire to have her think she is dying. He attempts to control her life and death, just as the four libertines of Sade's *120 Days of Sodom* control the lives of their victims.

The only way the writer Katherine Mortenhoe can triumph over the producer, refuse to become his object, is to take the plot into her own hands, as did the storyteller of *120 Days of Sodom*, the only person besides the four Libertines to come out alive. By taking over the plot, Katherine becomes the subject, transforming the producer into her object. By committing suicide, she reveals him to the witnesses for what he is, a sadistic murderer instead of a triumphant hero. The self-destructive nature of the power structure is also revealed. The only way he can triumph is to make her revolt against death, that is, him. The entire drama of the television series is annihilated in this revolt. The only way for her to affirm her own identity and defeat him is to commit suicide—destroy herself to destroy him. Sade's storyteller lived.

When Roddy is accidentally caught in a workers' battle, the policeman explains he is perhaps picking on him because he detests "city people, their arrogance, their power." So Roddy is thrown in jail to satisfy a cop's sense of power. Left in the dark, Roddy risks becoming blind, the camera batteries dying. Thus he, too, truly feels like an object.

The producer asks Roddy's wife Tracy to have a drink with him and gloats over the success of the series. Tracy asks him why he does it and he says, "oh it's not for money." "Then why? the power?" He changes the subject to avoid answering. Awaiting their drinks she asks, "Aren't there others who find that obscene, sickening?" He replies with the statistic: "Yes, thirty-seven percent find it unpleasant, but they still watch. Me, too."

Of the power he thought he had, the producer says to Tracy, "Do you realize that from one moment to the next, everything can fall apart?" Tracy replies, "For you, perhaps." It can only backfire, destroy the participants in the game—those who have consented to participate in it.

Roddy explains to Katherine's first husband that he had not hesitated to give his eyesight in exchange for a camera, to be able to grasp everything he saw, to capture it on film forever: "the supreme toy," supreme because of the sense of power it gave him. Now that he is blind and Katherine dead, he realizes how little value that power had and is happy and grateful to reclaim his wife, having learned to appreciate caring, the emotion, as more important in life than public power.

Fresh Bait

Even when there is a real *fait divers* as the initial inspiration, the emotion is what the viewers remember, not the story or plot. The teenage girls find they can get paid a lot more going out with rich older men, thanks to an entrepreneurial bar owner, than they can make as sales clerks. The men are the ones in power, therefore they have the money to make objects of the girls who have grown up in that mental environment anyhow and merely see more money at their disposition. The two young male companions of the one girl, one of whom is her lover, are also looking for a way for enough money to live independently. Selling their bodies is not as lucrative as it is for females, but burglary is. If they could open a store in America, they could make it. To get the money for such an enterprise, they, too, use the body of the girlfriend. She will gain admission to rich men's apartments, leave the door open, and they will follow, tie up the man, and steal his money. Or such is their naive plot. The rich men do not keep cash in their apartment and the youth have not concealed their physical appearance well. As a consequence, they get almost no money and have to kill the men to get rid of witnesses, something they conceal from the girl as they know she cannot stand violence or the idea of killing others.

There is more plot than Tavernier usually uses, though it amounts to no more than an idea by youth to get rich fast. The characters are equally shallow to communicate how easily the ordinary young person can be corrupted by the social structure. Only the youthful innocence of their horrible enterprise retains our interest. The real shock comes at the end when the girl gives witness against the two youth and naively asks the inspector, "Will I be released by Christmas, because I'd like to see my father." Shock because the spectators are forced to ask the question, Where would the social system have taught her that it is a crime to take advantage of others? The men get by with taking advantage of her. Her parents are divorced; no one was home to take care of her. Why should she feel guilt? Suddenly the storyline is irrelevant. The emotional conflict generated in the spectators forces them to recognize they are part and parcel of a system that has degenerated to the point of freeing youth of any guilt for robbery, extorsion, or murder. A hierarchical power system with no effective brakes can only self-destruct eventually.

L.627

Tavernier was highly criticized from showing Arabs and Blacks as the drug dealers. But those immigrants find themselves on the lowest rung of the power ladder. They have little to lose by trafficking drugs and, as in the case of female prostitution, it pays a great deal more than the day labor jobs they could get. The film opens with some of them spray painting the cars they cannot afford, including the police's stake-out van.

The drug team tries to grab a major dealer; but an inebriated boss with a desk job demands the van; it is more important to him to have a van to get to bed than for the team to catch a big dealer. Because he revolts against this so-called superior, the cop in charge of the bust, Lulu, is demoted to a menial desk job in another unit. Having an old friend with connections in the new police station, he gets transferred to another narcotics team. "Dodo" is their boss, and, with the rest of the team as witnesses, loves beating on suspects with a newspaper or shooting them (and the team members) with a water pistol to demonstrate his superiority. The childishness of the structure is underscored by his behavior. His interest in his superior position prompts him many times to forego the group's objective and merely grab the most expedient suspect to contribute to the statistics he needs for advancement.

Captain Conan

The ultimate pursuit of power is inevitably war where sado-masochism is consummated. Destroy and be destroyed. Tavernier had always skirted the actual battlefield until this film. The actual battle inevitably seemed to lead to the glory of the winner. At first Captain Conan seems destined for the heroic. But his nightly triumphs of enemy sabotage are not the cause of the end of the war. Tavernier has selected a moment when the war is already coming to an end to show Conan and his chosen comrades in arms as butchers, not heroes. The other soldiers admired them when they were in battle and they happened to survive thanks to Conan's attacks. But when the *détente* occurs, Conan's band is the first to be prosecuted for the continued pillaging, murder, and theft that is perpetrated on the civilians, the society trying to live at peace. No one understands that the war itself turned these men into permanent butchers. In war, they had discovered a power over others, and above the law—Conan never follows orders; his men only follow his, not those of the military commanders—that gave them a sense of existing they had never experienced in the pre-war, mundane world. Conan had worked in his family's store that sold sewing notions before entering the military. After the exuberance experienced leading a band of "warriors" as he calls them, not fighters, he returns after the war to the local bar to drown himself, alone, with no witnesses to his former glory. Conan is the ultimate catastrophe of the pursuit for hierarchical power and its realization at the expense of others. He can succeed only so long as there are others he can legitimately kill.

The grenades and shots fired ahead of time are mere openers, allowing the men to approach the enemy close enough to attack brutally on a man-to-man basis, up close where they can see the eyes of the object they dominate, see the expression of fear, the recognition of their power: "Kill 'em all! No prisoners!" Conan cries. Then they return to the troops they just saved from such butchery at the hands of the enemy and receive the admiration and confirmation of that power by others. They are not so different from the military commanders themselves who are more interested in seeing their own orders followed than in the men themselves, more concerned by the recognition they get for their own power than by the success of their troops in battle.

The Lieutenant De Scève opens the film by venturing out into the trenches to console his men when shots are fired. For a moment, he appears to be our hero. Then Conan and his band scale the walls of the trenches without any of De Scève's guards spotting them. They continue immediately in the dark to attack the next hill and destroy the enemy post there, proudly returning with no prisoners, for they killed all. De Scève, in the meantime, has been discussing the lack of mutton. Back at camp, Conan takes wine to his wounded before joining the other officers for dinner. The major reprimands him and his companion, Lieutenant Norbert, for arriving late. Upon being served the meager potatoes eaten by the other officers, Conan excuses himself and Norbert, saying their stomachs have been upset by the hospital visit. They return to the quarters of his band where a delicious stew complete with olives and onions is being served his men, accompanied by a good Bordeaux. Conan's band never fails to take its due.

Conan is obeyed by his men because he takes care of them and covers up for their thefts by taking the blame on himself. Whereas the other troops, suffering from dysentery, are obliged to stand in the rain

at attention while the commanding officer announces the victory of the
French, Conan's band has been excused from the ceremony due to
illness. They are lounging comfortably under cover from the rain.

Lieutenant Norbert serves as the theme in counterpoint. He tries
to understand, not judge. When asked to act as attorney for accused
violators of military law, he tries to refuse, but accepts when he sees
how easily the other officers would condemn any who had been
reported to "serve as an example" for the others. Conan, alone with
Norbert later, mocks his charge, reading off some of the charges: "And
this colonial? three days to find his regiment. Get the picture? A
Bedouin lost among the Gypsies. At least he looked for his regiment."
Conan underscores Norbert dilemma: "How can these men be
condemned who are admirable companions in battle and at the same
time assassins of women?" Both he and Conan understand the humans
caught in the war. Conan, however, revels in the sense of existing he
gets from the exercise of power; Norbert just tries to understand.

The difference in their approach is seen when they are dealing with
their men, whether Conan's band or Norbert's accused. The director
of the girl's school where Conan's men are lodged complains because
the band stole a side of pork intended for all and roasted it in their
quarters. The group complains they are bored. Conan immediately
orders them into uniform and parades them out of their quarters, past
the commanding officer—explaining this is a "punitive drill"—and
straight to the local bordello. The problem is apparently solved, though
they end up behaving so badly in the bordello—killing one woman,
paralyzing another, and stealing all the money—that Norbert has Conan
sent on a mission to prevent him from accepting all the blame and
being court-martialed to cover up for his men. During the raid, Conan
protects his chosen female who says after the excitement is over,
"Well, I didn't come for nothing!" to which Conan replies: "Neither
did they." He recognized and understood the brutality of his men who
had come to take their just rewards.

Norbert, on the other hand, gets his accused released from charges
by pleading their situation with such humor that they are never
punished. One soldier has been accused of stealing a farmer's chicken:
he was hungry. Faced with one of Conan's band whom he knows was
one of the assassins of the woman at the nightclub and the one who
stole the money, he is confounded when the accused rips off one of his
medals and throws it before him saying, "And that too I must have
stolen." The spectator who witnessed both his heroic attacks and the

nightclub robbery is forced to understand the dilemma along with Norbert. Judgment is no longer so easy. When we find Lieutenant De Scève more interested in upholding military law according to the letter rather than the spirit—he shows no understanding or compassion for his physically weak relative—he appears at least as criminal as Conan and his band.

The only one who does not end up alone, alienated from the rest of the world by the end of the film, is Norbert. The heroes of battle no longer have any justification for their existence. Neither the miliary officers nor the terrorist band can find the subservient reactions in others that gave them their glorified meaning during the war. Norbert goes on, a teacher, just trying to understand his students. His sense of identity never changed. That of Conan was plunged into a void. The actual military rendition of the hierarchical power struggle clearly shows its ultimate self-destructive nature.

In all his films, Tavernier subtly or blatantly caricatures the power structure, therein breaching its walls. The spectators always go away with their respect for those in power seriously undermined in one field or another. Their emotions have been stirred and they have gained an understanding of an individual who is being sacrificed for someone else's self-glorification.

Notes

1. According to Sade's character, Father Clément, in *Justine*, 1969, 166-71.

2. Garrity 1984, 56-60; I disagree with Garrity that this scene causes us to reject our previous identification with Cordier. On the contrary, because of our previous sympathy for Cordier, we become appropriately indignant over the exercise of power.

3. Quotations in the following film analyses are from the film under discussion unless otherwise noted.

5

Towards Complexity

Transforming Prejudices

Tavernier's originality lies in his ability to transform the spectators' judgment about a number of characters between the beginning and the end of the film. In most Hollywood films, we know who the good guys and the bad guys are within the first fifteen minutes; our interest is retained merely by the curiosity of finding out how the good guys are going to get out of a bad situation and punish the bad guys. That requires a causal plot. In a Tavernier film, we have one opinion of the characters after the first fifteen minutes, and then the rest of the film is devoted to unsettling our opinion until, at the end, we have a more open mind and are trying to understand rather than have a set opinion or judgment.

We have just seen how Tavernier reverses our opinion several times in *Clean Slate*. Though the first reversal—when we begin to like Cordier for his slaughter of the *salauds*—could be said to come from the withholding of information, as in Hitchcock's *Psycho*. But the final one comes from our witnessing his execution of Friday, and no information has been withheld at all. Generally, Tavernier's reversals are not due to a withholding of information, a classic trick of comedy, but from a revelation of the complexity of the characters' social relationships, our judgment turning from the individual character to the entire social structure in which we, the spectators, take part.

At the beginning of *Daddy Nostalgia*, when news arrives that the father has just had a stroke, the daughter-writer immediately departs for the hospital in the south of France. The initial impression is that of a very loving daughter and of a close father-daughter relationship. During recovery, they sneak out together to bars and appear to be inseparable. In the end, just before she departs to take care of her own child (whom she left in the care of her husband from whom she has separated), she confirms, with a loving smile: you were a terrible father, a fact he has just acknowledged himself. We realize he only became loving on his deathbed. There is no explanation or justification in the film; the audience is made to discover this opposition by flashbacks within or between scenes. Family obligations, paternal prerogatives, and especially the male's right to ego gratification have been questioned. Without any direct criticisms or analysis presented in the film, the viewer is left with various questions, such as, "How can fathers justify their self-indulgences when their children need them?" or, "Why does society expect children to grieve or look after parents who totally ignored them when they needed their love and care?" Another sister in the family fled to Montreal. There is one apparently condemning comment early in the film that seems to blame her for paying little attention to her parents. By the end of the film, she seems exonerated, for they obviously paid little attention to either daughter when young. The daughter-writer's problem seems to remain, even after her father's death; she is still in search of that paternal love she never received.

Throughout *Deathwatch* we see Katherine's feelings through the camera eyes of Roddy, which reveal a gloomy Glasgow and gloomier feelings, feelings that eventually become so guilt-ridden for Roddy that he goes blind. Then Katherine leads him to her first husband's (Max von Sydow's) house, resplendent with light and happiness. For the first time we see the world through Katherine's eyes, Roddy now being blind. The tonality of the set prevents her suicide from appearing to be a consequence of despair. Combined with the music she has requested that her ex-husband play, she seems to die triumphant, successfully defying the media's attempt to tell the story of her death. For the first time, Katherine wears a light-colored dress and sunlight basks the sets—the only two days of sunlight the crew saw during the entire shoot (Audé et al. 1980, 62). Here again, the setting, characters, and action are fully integrated, so much so that the reversal in tonality and point of view forces the spectators to question their own voyeurism. Whereas we began the film intrigued by the idea of watching someone die, we end disgusted by the fact that we might really pay to watch someone agonize—for we have just sat, fascinated, through a long film doing just that.

In the beginning of *Beatrice*, the spectator is touched by the daughter's kindness and innocence, and though she has moments of impetuous anger, she seems young for such responsibilities, so we forgive her. Then we are horrified by the brutality and vulgarity of her father upon his return. He is a murderer, rapist, arsonist, brigand and more. Yet by the end of the film, we, too, have accepted murder as the only way out for Beatrice. The film successfully sets us up to see the hierarchical power structure as self-destructive and self-defeating and makes us desire its collapse by wishing the death of François de Cortemare, not so much out of hatred of him—for he has come to appear almost pathetic—but because Beatrice has no other way out.

L.627 reads as a documentary told from the point of view of a day-to-day cop charged with the drug busts. What Tavernier destroys using this point of view is the bourgeois comfort that there is a law force out there taking care of the problems and that we can forget about it, as long as it is out of sight. He exposes the system of valued social acts at the heart of the hierarchical system as little more than statistics. The cop Lulu, trying sincerely to address the drug problem, is actually prevented from doing so by the system itself that rewards cops based on the number of arrests, regardless of their social value. As a consequence, Lulu, who is trying to catch the supplier of the drugs and employs the users to get information, finds all his efforts come to naught when the supervisor decides to bust a bunch of users to increase the numbers of arrests made. All of Lulu's informants are now behind bars and the supplier, of course, is still at large. That the film was condemned by the French Minister of the Interior for being a caricature is proof that it struck at the system successfully. The representative of the largest civil police union in Europe said the film "dispensed him from making his annual moral report because in it was everything all the policemen were screaming in silence and that the politicians refuse to hear" (Bonneville 1993, 16). When Tavernier spoke to the First Minister, Laurent Fabius, about the reality of the drug situation, about the sale of drugs in front of schools, he was cut short by the cliché: "Wait a moment, I asked you to speak to me about important things!" (B.B. and D.R.-B 1992, 56). Tavernier made the film in response to that remark, one that typifies the *status quo par excellence*, the desire of those in power to avoid upsetting the apple-cart no matter what.

In *The Clockmaker* Tavernier does not try to make us identify with any of the characters, but rather understand. Like the father Michel, we learn to reject the facile psychologizing that justifies the murder for the lawyer and the police. Instead, we are forced to reconstruct, as does Michel, his son's murderous act with respect for the social, historical and personal context; we try to understand Bernard and his father rather than trying to make them what society thinks a person should be.

In *Life and Nothing But* Tavernier succeeds in captivating the audience with its prejudices in place and then making the spectators feel uncomfortable with their own position because their opinion, their feeling about the character, has been altered during the film. In the beginning, Noiret as the major appears cold and calculating as he classifies the dead. By the end, he seems much more sensitive and feeling than any of the other military or politicians awarding honors. By honoring one unknown soldier they can get the public to forget the 1.4 million dead. His figures suddenly seem more human than history. The method used for selecting the unknown soldier from the six coffins at the ceremony appears ludicrous and inhuman: we learn that Corporal Thain, the only historical character in the film besides the Minister Maginot whose mission was to designate November 10, 1920, as a patriotic day in France, uses coincidences of the number six (his serial numbers add up to six, for example) to place the floral bouquet on the sixth casket. In the beginning, Irene represents a spoiled high-class bitch and by the end she reveals herself as warm and understanding, her manners appearing more the fault of the pretentious society in which she was reared than inherent in her. But then she herself has had her blinders removed by her understanding of Dellaplane.

In *A Sunday in the Country* at first we empathize entirely with the father as an older man neglected by his family, relatively abandoned. Then we discover that the son, in many ways the father's image—unadventurous, preferring bourgeois security—dearly seeks his father's approval, but gets none. The father sees his own failure to pursue a truly original art path reflected in his son's choice of a secure office career and consequently projects his self-loathing onto the son. His daughter, favored because she dares to do everything he never did but wanted to do, arrives like a breath of fresh air, and we really do not blame him for preferring such a lively individual. Yet she is censured for not spending enough time with her father. By the end of the film, all our judgments are suspended.

Society would agree that she should take more time to be with her father; but we feel what a bore that would be; the son is the obedient one by society's standards, but how dull he is; and the proverbial father isn't without his sins any longer either. We rather blame him for not

having had his own adventures and taking that failure out on his son
and his family. Yet what we have is to some degree the situation of
every normal family faced with the care of an older person. There is
always one sibling preferred to another; one sibling who reflects a
parent's limitations and is therefore an uncomfortable mirror. Our
earlier impressions have been tempered, and any spectators who have
had a family or career, and at the same time an aging single parent,
find the conflicting emotions and social obligations of their lives within
the film.

In *The Judge and the Assassin*, we are horrified at first by
Bouvier's rapes, disembowelments, and acts of sodomy of twelve- to
fifteen-year-old boys and girls. And we are just as indignant as the
judge. Then we learn Bouvier used to be a sergeant in the military.
Later the magistrates admit he is quite sane enough to fight in a war,
but they do not have a war for him to fight. Bouvier blames society and
by the end of the film, we no longer find it easy to distinguish black
from white. The film ends with the people revolting against the powers
that be and we are given the statistics of the 2,500 children who died
in coal mines versus Bouvier's twelve, but no one is punishing the
entrepreneurs who send the children into the mines. Absolute judgment
is put in question and understanding asked for. What techniques has
Tavernier used to bring about this change in the spectator—and our
opinion of the characters?

(1) Conflict between the ones in power and the hunted. The viewer
at first recognizes the approved social and religious values in the judge
and disapproves, out of social conformity if nothing else, Bouvier's
criminal acts. But as the relationship is explored, we come to dislike
more and more the judge's absolute assurance regarding what is right
and wrong. At the same time we discover a few sympathetic traits in
Galabru; he becomes more human as the judge becomes less so.

(2) Then when the judge begins to imitate the behavior of Galabru,
we can no longer completely approve or condemn one or the other.

(a) Both seek the approval of women.

(b) The judge, in the end, cannot control his natural instincts
any better than Bouvier. After one of his meetings with the
assassin, the judge runs to his mistress and sodomizes her at the
kitchen table.

(c) Both seek fame and public acclaim.

(d) Both depend on Bouvier's murders to achieve their goal:
Bouvier to get his picture in the papers and Judge Rousseau to get

documentation on tramps that will make him an expert on the subject.

(e) If the judge is unafraid of Bouvier until physically attacked, Bouvier is never impressed by the judge's position or money, never subjugated by his persona.

Understanding has replaced judgment. At the same time, the judgmental values of the spectators' own culture seem less certain, less right. Now they, too, are subject to questioning and no longer provide comforting assurance.

Captain Conan and his band at first appear more heroic than the regular army, actually rescuing the latter several times. By the end of the film, however, the continued will to kill even though the enemy has retreated, combined with the willful destruction of property and murder committed by the band when not in battle, leads us to question the nature of heroism. The uselessness of such battles, epitomized in the senseless death of a young volunteer totally lost and terrified in the midst of battle, seems to outweigh the need for any heroes. Nothing about Conan appears heroic in his life after the war. Once again Tavernier has exposed our own prejudices regarding heroes.

Open Endings

Tavernier does not conclude, though his films are esthetically complete. His endings remain open to the spectators' interpretation and to exploration of new solutions for the social problems revealed. He said, "I didn't want to program audience reactions. I am upset to see how manipulative so many movies are these days" (Coursodon 1986, 23). Many of the endings in a Tavernier film seem arbitrary, and he has been criticized because they do not seem motivated by the plot (Forbes 1992, 162), as though there were but one possible conclusion for all the gratuitous and unforeseen encounters that enter into a life! Tavernier, showing a society on "the edge of chaos," gives us an ending just as likely as many others, given the numerous conflicting forces at work. *The Judge and the Assassin* has an ending proclaiming the revolution, and Tavernier was immediately criticized because it seemed artificial. An appropriate criticism perhaps since it is set in the eighteenth century, just as Laclos' *Liaisons dangereuses* was criticized for the same reason when he had Mme. de Merteuil come down with smallpox and lose her fortune as punishment for her meddling. Yet every modern

Figure 16: Home for Christmas.   *Fresh Bait*

adaption of it has had a completely different ending, becoming more
and more open to the spectator's interpretation.

"There is neither a lesson nor a user's manual" in *L.627*.
"Everything remains open, including the personal relationship of the
characters. . . . I wanted this open ending which questions the
spectators. It is a way of saying: now it is up to you to continue the
film; it belongs to you" (Bonneville 1993, 16). At the end Lulu and his
wife may be separating, but we cannot be sure. He encounters a former
prostitute, Cécile, HIV-positive, whom he had helped get off drugs;
then he lost track of her. Now she has a baby and is about to move to
the country. After he fortuitously runs into her when on a stake-out,
Lulu has to rejoin his team, only to realize he never got Cécile's new
address.

In *Fresh Bait*, Nathalie's boyfriend and his buddy decide to use her
to get access to men's apartments to rob. Finally the police come for
them, but need her to tell them what happened. She eventually
acquiesces, saying she knew nothing about the murders. The film closes
with her confession as she, in all innocence, asks the inspector if she
will be released in time for Christmas, because she "would like to go
see her father" (figure 16). The effect on the spectators is like an

Figure 17: The Blank Canvas.   *A Sunday in the Country*

ending in the Theater of the Absurd. They have not arrested the bar
owner who sold her. The men who paid are dead, of course, but they
are deemed the rightful victims. In a society run by that kind of male
permissiveness, why should a young female teenager think she is
responsible for the consequences? They wanted to buy; they were just
expected to pay more than the bar-owner took. The spectators cannot
help but be embarrassed by their acceptance of the social mores to
which she fell prey.

In the end of *A Sunday in the Country* M. Ladmiral is alone and
facing a blank canvas (figure 17). An extraordinarily moving ending,
it is pregnant with possibilities, but no answers. Perhaps he will paint
the girls skipping rope that he noted with pleasure twice during his
walks.

Life and Nothing But ends with Irene, about to leave for the United
States to get away from her family and French upper-class bourgeois
values for which she no longer has any great esteem, as she reads the
letter she has received from Major Dellaplane, who has retired to his
country estate and is inviting her to share the rest of his life with him
and declaring his love for her. The film ends there. Will she return or
did he miss his chance?

'*Round Midnight* would have been complete with the announcement of Dale's death to Francis. It would also have seemed closed to interpretation. Tavernier reopens it by playing the video Francis had made of Dale and his daughter on a beach, with the voice-over of Dale. Tavernier tells us, "The lines were not in the script. At the end of the shoot, I went to the studio with Dexter, and I made him talk about certain things. . . . I had written something which he had told me one day. 'I hope that one day there will be—*the parks and the streets named after great jazz musicians.*' He did it. He recorded it. And I suddenly asked him, without preparing it . . . 'What about Dale Turner?' And he looked at me, surprised, but immediately he said, 'Maybe a street called Dale Turner.' . . . I had the ending" (Dempsey 1987, 4). Now the film is open to reflection by the spectators.

Tavernier's films do not judge, they remain open to development and interpretation. For critics who think their job is to judge rather than reveal or elucidate films, Tavernier is open to criticism (e.g., Stanley Kauffmann's reviews in the *New Republic*) because his films never make a point. For Tavernier, that would constitute a closure, a frozen form, whereas his entire enterprise is to dismantle the frozen forms that prevent society from finding new possibilities and solutions for human relationships. These open endings constitute the final *coup* to traditional storyline and traditional film critics who seek narrative at all cost as the only possible filmic experience.

In Tune with the Twentieth Century

Tavernier continually succeeds in changing the viewers' prejudices, opening up minds to new interpretations, and suspending judgments. By fracturing the causal plot progression, he permits evolution to occur. All great artists succeed in breaching some part or parts of the frozen mold preventing change. Writers have been chipping away at the hierarchical power structure since the eighteenth century at least.[1] When they tried before that, they were imprisoned. Film, however, is an art form for the masses. The costs of production, even Tavernier's modest ones, require a mass audience. As a result, most films, especially those of profit-hungry Hollywood producers, reinforce the standard mold. They are guaranteed to be understood by everyone. Stephen Spielberg succeeded in questioning the power structure with *E.T.* only because he used children and fantasy to do so. That did give

him the right to direct as he pleased *Schindler's List*, dealing with the
Holocaust, which no one dreamed would become a financial success.
The linear storyline there is equally irrelevant; all spectators know the
outcome before the film begins. The spectators' interest is held for
three hours by the business clichés Schindler is using to surreptitiously
obtain the Jewish prisoners from the Germans. Every time we hear the
business proposition he is using, always one sanctioned by the power
structure (such as: "Jewish labor is cheaper than local laborers, so I
can make you a better price"), we simultaneously hope the Germans
will not discover the truth behind the cliché and are confounded that the
cliché can be used for what the Germans believe to be "their
advantage" in war. The film can easily be read as an attack on
America's monetary power structure. There are a few more modest
Hollywood productions, such as *A River Runs Through It*, that also use
realistic adult settings to question the structure.

French cinema has a long history of questioning the power
structure. All of the Prévert-Carné films of the 1930s do it. Tavernier
appropriately dedicates one of his to Prévert. Buñuel's entire career
proved an embarrassment to the establishment. Jean Renoir's *Rules of
the Game* (1939) flagrantly mocks the established power structure that
brought World War I to France, and it mocked it on the very eve of
World War II. Almost all New Wave filmmakers also question the
structure. Tavernier appears to be less revolutionary than they because
of his use of realism. He achieves even more dramatic results, perhaps,
fighting fire with fire. Hooked into an all-too-familiar world, the
viewers are not merely prompted to question bourgeois practices. By
the end of most of his films, at least one bourgeois prejudice has been
exploded, removed. Viewers are embarrassed to have thought and felt
as they did before seeing the film, including their preference for the
socially, politically, or economically successful individuals, regardless
of their character.

Tavernier's techniques demonstrate that breaking out of the
limitations imposed by the hierarchical power structure demands
breaking down the walls constructed by linear narrative. Like Renoir
before him, Tavernier not only uses the long shot but cinema scope as
well to express the importance of mankind coming together regardless
of racial or social differences.

Consonant with current theories of Chaos or Complexity,
Tavernier's films recognize that evolution cannot take place without
fracturing the fixed sociopolitical mold. In the nineteenth century,

Gustave Flaubert complained that nothing had changed since the Middle Ages. The names at the top and bottom of the hierarchical power structure changed, but after every revolution, the same structure reappeared. When the first *Internationale* met, the elitist Flaubert was ecstatic: finally a real change! One month later, the disillusionment had set in. Communism was just another new name with different people at the top and others dwindling towards the bottom.

The power structure had to achieve the horrors of the Holocaust and the A-bomb before its self-destructive nature became politically evident. The Marquis de Sade's works that said the same thing were banned until World War II. Afterwards, history had surpassed any of the horrors Sade described to make the readers revolt against the power structure. Those devoted to protecting the power structure could not ban history as they had Sade, and he was finally published.

Tavernier's techniques for fracturing the mold are particularly successful. True of any period of major change and transition, similar and related phenomena occur elsewhere. In the 1960s, several movements coalesce, situating Tavernier in what is, perhaps, the mainstream of ideas that define the late twentieth century, ideas that fundamentally have two thrusts. On the one hand, movements in all fields have stressed the patterns or relationships between things, people, or words as more defining than the historical development of any one individual. Simultaneously, others, and sometimes the same, have considered the ruptures in those patterns as necessary for evolution or change, the latter validating the importance of the first.

Nietzsche and Flaubert are examples of originators of such thinking. Nietzsche's insistence on the Dionysian principle of chaos and the Apollonian one of order shows the latter as limiting evolution, preventing a strong individual from fully living all the possibilities of being, reaffirming that which is already known. *Madame Bovary* was Flaubert's expression of ultimate disgust with the hierarchical power structure he found so stifling because it never changed and kept limiting exploration of any new form of thought. An example of his attempt to rupture its shell is the agricultural fair scene where he juxtaposes the sacred principles of awards with the equally insipid language of romantic seduction, showing them both to be the same form: the powerful (the government and the male) seduce the weak (the hard-working farmers and the female) with promises of blue ribbons and happiness in order to exploit them for all they are worth.

Studies of nonlinear system dynamics (or Chaos Theory) were

launched in the very early years of this century by the mathematician Henri Poincaré. In the 1960s, Mitchell Feigenbaum and others used computers to explore patterns in the physical world that humans had not had the patience to calculate. The American Stuart Kauffman presents a theory of biological evolution that modifies Darwin's theory. According to his *At Home in the Universe* (1995), a book for the general public that summarizes thirty years of his scientific work—the more scientific version appearing in *The Origins of Order* (1993)—evolution is limited by self-organization. Being the fittest no longer suffices to bring about evolution after a frozen form has established itself. Breaches in the walls of that form are necessary to permit new forms, ideas, and events to be entertained as real and allowed to mature. Breaking the frozen form to try the unexplored is known as living on "the edge of chaos."

Kauffman's theory and others dealing with Complexity or Chaos Theory are easily transported to literature where Proust planted similar seeds to those of Poincaré, Proust himself having been inspired in part by Poincaré (see my *Chaos Theory, Complexity, Cinema and the Evolution of the French Novel*). Proust thoroughly fractured the concept of causal development by introducing seemingly arbitrary and often trivial events as important factors in an individual's decisions. Swann was introduced to Odette as someone she was not, and, pursuing that illusion, experiences an anguish that becomes so familiar to him he cannot give it up and thus he marries her. And Swann's love story is the most traditional part of *Remembrance of Things Past*, the rest of the novel playing against it, showing even more relative developments of social and political events. But great novelists have always chipped away at the frozen forms defining the power structure. Indeed, the novel as an art form could be defined as just that since it alone had no rules. In the twentieth century, the more avant-garde novelists, whether Proust, Kafka, Faulkner, or Joyce, have trashed the causal development that supported the power structure in order to expose it as limiting.

Following on their heels, Noam Chomsky and Ferdinand Saussure turned the attention of linguistics to the structure or patterns of things as more significant than the content or historical (linear) development of a culture or phoneme. The way words came together were more expressive than an individual word or its history alone. Patterns of usage reflected the culture using the language. Claude Lévi-Strauss started a related movement in anthropology in the 1950s and 1960s. By insisting that our concepts of reality were determined by cultural patterns that imposed an apparent order on nature, he turned the interest to the patterns as defining rather than the historical development as doing so.

At approximately the same time, Michel Foucault notes the relativity of structures or forms to our body of knowledge comprised of the ready-made concepts of previous generations. *The Order of Things* traces the changes in these general truths from the Classical period to the present, with the interrelationships, the processes that generate structures, replacing the interest static structures acquired earlier and which had replaced the concern with the value of a thing itself. Foucault notes that each age, coming to an end—the transitional period, or what modern scientists are calling "the edge of chaos"—has had an exemplary literary character performing according to the approved form of the old order, but revealing the emptiness of that structure, such as Don Quixote at the point of transition between the Renaissance and Classicism and, he suggests, Sade's *Justine* and *Juliette* at the moment of transition between Classicism and Romanticism. Sade's sated libertines are playing out the forms, the representation of desire, but, in fact, have no real desire. The aristocratic hierarchical structure according them privileges has locked them into its form, allowing them no chance for exploration. Sade and Don Quixote express ruptures that make change possible; ruptures, not causal development.

The nineteenth century proceeded to look at the organic structure of things, that is, not just the shape itself, but the way it functions, grows, the way one part affects another and the interrelationships between those parts. Analogies become useful referents associating things that have no external similarity. Such a change allows for a new hierarchy, that of the bourgeoisie, to come to the fore. Labor has taken a place in the sociopolitical system as a force to be accorded recognition. A working individual may acquire social and political status and rank by virtue of his earned wealth. For Foucault, this coincides with an understanding in the modern world of the inter-dependence of one organ on another, namely, that one organ cannot function properly without the functioning of another. This is as true of bodily functions as of social, political, and economic functions.

In the 1960s, movements in literature and film—movements in the arts used to materialize in Paris, spreading in bits and pieces to other countries—took a blatant stance against the frozen forms being perpetuated by the reigning bourgeois hierarchical power structure.

Many did it with subject matter, which does not really breach the walls of frozen forms. Céline and Queneau used socially unacceptable language to write their novels. Louis Malle's film, *The Lover*, scandalized the French because it depicted a well-to-do woman leaving her secure, elegant marriage and running off with a young man with whom she has fallen in love. In the 1960s, that behavior was something only the shopgirls and prostitutes of literature did. Malle shocked more with the subject matter than with the form.

The French New Novelists attacked the form of discourse itself, as had Proust and Joyce. They were no longer the exception, but the rule. Many used the detective story turned upside down. Starting with what should have been the solution to a murder or other dilemma, the story then proceeds to investigate, to learn about past events from different perspectives in the present, concluding that there had not been an event at all, or that the real problem is totally different from the one that received a conclusion or solution. Robbe-Grillet's novels typically follow this format, but so does Butor's *La Modification* (*Change of Heart*).

The New Wave movement in film had a visible impact on cinema even in Hollywood. Before the movement, the studio ruled supreme. The public knew only the names of the stars. Directors' names were rarely mentioned. Since the New Wave, directors' names have become not only as well known as that of the stars, Robert Redford being known as both, and others, such as Steven Spielberg, having their own production company, DreamWorks SKG. Universal Pictures won at the Oscars with *Schindler's List* only because it had accorded Spielberg total autonomy over the production. More and more American directors are demanding various degrees of that autonomy in their contracts, allowing them to venture outside the confines of the frozen structure. Independent filmmakers, not Hollywood studios, now reign supreme at the Oscars. That in itself constitutes a major breach in the hierarchical power structure of which Hollywood studios are undoubtedly the supreme example.

The characteristics of independent films that are winning are also those of New Wave films. Stars and glamor are not essential to the success of a film, nor are spectacular events or even great plot: *Secrets and Lies*, for example. Personal emotion as the result of everyday problems becomes more important, as the main spokesman of the New Wave, François Truffaut, had eloquently proclaimed.[2]

Jean-Luc Godard makes films to contest every traditional mode of cinematic expression precisely because that mode supports and sustains the frozen form of bourgeois values. His first feature, *Breathless*, is a take-off on the gangster genre. How does the gangster tradition support bourgeois values, the frozen form? In gangster films, there is always a black get-away car. Gangsters in films are rarely so poor that they do not own or have access to a fast car for an escape. In *Breathless*, the gangster Michel first steals a white sports car then a big white Cadillac convertible—in a city where, at the time, all other cars were still brown or black. Both cars underscore the importance of material gain that dominates gangster films as well as the frozen social form.

A woman is always dependent on the gangster and he can always hide at her place. The opposite occurs in *Breathless* where the gangster Michel steals from one working-class girl he knows and has to break into Patricia's room when she is away in order to gain admittance. She supports herself selling the *New York Herald Tribune* and ends up turning him over to the police rather than sacrifice her budding, independent career in journalism. Godard's satire of the genre itself is a satire of the bourgeois frozen form where career advancement is more important than a personal relationship.

Alain Resnais' use of juxtapositions inspired by both the comics and surrealism, shocked the cinematic world as destroying and questioning the bourgeois form, for it questioned the linear, causal, sequential way it perceives itself. In *Last Year at Marienbad*, a man picks up a married woman at a spa by inventing a story about meeting last year. They could never have met last year, nonetheless, the invented story generates a relationship between them that becomes quite real. The film therein questions the need for any real story as the basis of film, creating its own story merely by inventing a fake one. *Hiroshima, Mon Amour* generates another love, the emotion of it, by juxtaposing a chance encounter in the present in Hiroshima with the memory of a German soldier from World War II who was her lover when she was sixteen, a love that was destroyed when he was shot and she was subsequently banned by the French as a collaborator. The juxtaposition of the two stories questions the basis for wars, wars claiming to defend ones nation against an aggressor. Excuses for aggression are always those that are sanctioned by bourgeois values: the supremacy of a given race; the superiority of a hero and his right to lead others into battle "for the good of the country"—usually defined as economic good, but disguised by the country's favorite values, whether freedom, righteousness, or defense of the mistreated. Resnais' juxtapositions seriously challenged storytelling as a mode of communication. Robert Aldrich is one of the few American directors who has dared follow a similar path, which explains why Bertrand Tavernier is a particular fan of his.

Notes

1. See my book, *Chaos Theory, Complexity, Cinema and the Evolution of the French Novel* (Lewiston, N.Y.: The Edwin Mellen Press, 1996).

2. Consult the numerous interviews published in Bazin et al., *La politique des auteurs*, 1972.

6

Tips for a New Cinema

Hollywood's action effects have been exploited to the limit, to the point where another entertainment film is just a variation of explosions and automobile (bus, truck, plane) chases. Furthermore, the cost of such films has become so staggering that one has to question their social responsibility—are they justified for the sake of pure entertainment?

The significant rise in independent films receiving major awards is indicative of a growing public's desire for more content than effects, for a cinema that touches their own life rather than helping them escape it for only a couple of hours. Tavernier's films provide a valuable resource, lessons, and techniques for filmmakers seeking to tap into this interest. The fundamental objective becomes the opening of new horizons in the viewer's everyday life. To achieve this, the inherent prejudices of the viewer must be shattered so that new solutions and relationships can be discovered. This objective and the necessity for changing the way people think were current concepts in art in the late nineteenth century. The eighteenth-century writer tentatively pursued the same path, often paying for the attempt with years in prison. As we move into the twenty-first century, anyone who is not pursuing that avenue is truly behind the times. Tavernier's enterprise provides some positive indications of visual means that can help accomplish this in cinema.

In general Tavernier defies narrative traditions because the causal logic supports the reigning ideology. We could summarize the major paths his work takes thusly:

(1) Historical subject matter from periods in transition provides a

wealth of reflective material, reflective in the sense that it contains
many aspects of our own traumas that are perceived more objectively
from a distance. Viewers, too embroiled in contemporary problems,
consider suggestions for a solution to be personal and fail to perceive
them objectively. Few individuals consider their own prejudices, such
as a hierarchical manner of behavior or thought, as contemptible or
destructive. François de Cortemare's behavior is instinctively repulsive
to the spectators (I hope), yet they only become uneasy with their own
hierarchical behavior as they begin to have some understanding of the
man who had been left without a father at a young age.

(2) By exploiting the story of the uncelebrated individuals in
history, Tavernier reveals the plight of the ordinary man, much like
that of the spectators. Heroes and heroines have been replaced by
ordinary school teachers (*Clean Slate*), a mediocre reporter
(*Deathwatch*), or a not too attentive daughter (*A Sunday in the
Country*). Everyman and society's marginal characters (Bouvier)
become the principal actors. By providing a social context, implicit in
the set, they become as believable as our own neighbors.

(3) The power of the everyday event or object to engage the
spectators in the film as having a pertinence to their own world is
instrumental in transforming the viewers' prejudices. Because the scene
is so ordinary—for its time in history, at least—the viewers accept the
initial reaction dictated by their prejudices. Only as they become
uncomfortable with what is happening do they begin to question those
prejudices as their own. *Clean Slate* or *The Judge and the Assassin* are
supreme examples.

(4) Emotion replaces the climax or conclusion of a plot. For many
this may be the most puzzling. How do you generate emotion without
great characters and plot? Tavernier proves that the latter two elements
are part of our inherited cultural prejudices. He has shown that
suspense and interest, one of the apparent justifications for plot and
heroes, can be sustained by use of the butterfly effect, wherein an
inconsequential detail has major consequences—the camera eyes
implanted in the reporter's eyes (*Deathwatch*), the gun that is bought
so Rose can protect herself, or the evening the police chief spends in
the Bourkassa house of prostitution (*Clean Slate*).

Contrapuntal scenes also sustain our interest, focusing on crosscurrents of a present without a past to explain or justify events and
people, as in *'Round Midnight* or *The Clockmaker*. Parallels—whether
in actions, words, or characters—capture our attention. The

clockmaker's revolt is not so different from his son's. Multiple points of view and different levels of narration place the spectators in the middle, constantly trying to clarify the misunderstandings of the characters who cannot see the different viewpoints and meanings.

(5) Dialogue never explains what is happening. Often the viewers perceive that what one person says is not what another understands. They are forced to understand why two individuals cannot comprehend the same thing from the same words or events. But could they explain? Having become witnesses, are they not the guilty ones?

(6) And what about structure? What holds it together as a unified work of art if there is no beginning, middle, or end? Just as great classical works had a unified tone, color, sets, and rhythm, so do modern works, cinematic or otherwise. In modern works, however, those elements are no longer secondary to plot. They have come to the fore as in *Sunday in the Country*, *'Round Midnight*, *Beatrice*, or almost any of Tavernier's films.

Whereas these characteristics are now of primary importance, parallels in events or characters—parallels often causally unrelated, such as the clockmaker's relative who made matches illegally, the clockmaker's refusal to obey orders during the war, and the clockmaker's son's murder—provide a secondary set of events that have the appearance of action, but essentially buttress the emotional build-up of a film.

Of course other filmmakers have worked with these elements, but few have succeeded as well as Tavernier in transforming the social prejudices of the viewers, rupturing the closed frozen structures, opening up dialogue, and hopefully permitting renewed social evolution. Any film that fractures narrative only reaches a public capable of actively participating in a film. Active participation involves bringing one's own life experience to the film as it is being viewed. This habit, quite common in Europe, is unfortunately becoming increasingly rare in the United States. Television denies it, Hollywood will have nothing to do with it with rare exceptions, and our educational system does less of it. Worse, the mania for Hollywood entertainment films is spreading to other countries. The frozen forms are guaranteed a long future.

Young filmmakers seeking new horizons must find ways to engage the spectators sufficiently to break open their frozen forms of thought and at the same time provoke them to bring their own experiences to the film they are seeing, teach them how to relate to the world about them, a daunting task that should have been achieved by our educational and cultural systems: that is, teach individuals to think. In America, we have failed so miserably in this respect that we must look to the great tradition of French films for inspiration. The French were the first to recognize that film as a genre already had a past to build on—the New Wave films—and that it was time to explore new avenues if the genre were to evolve. The world is so used to dynamic French schools of artistic change providing a manifesto, such as the numerous proclamations of the New Wave directors, that when a truly unique artist such as Tavernier comes along, his originality is misunderstood, or worse, as in the United States, overlooked. Jean Renoir is one past example, now recognized as one of the masters of cinema. Tavernier offers a similar example. Like Renoir, he brings out the creative side of the actors and technicians to fabricate a work that surpasses that of any one individual, yet still bears the director's stamp. As unpretentious as Renoir, just as dedicated to his profession, and often similarly misunderstood, Tavernier offers a resource of inspiration, clues, and techniques for exploration, celebrating film as a truly communal enterprise that brings mankind together.

7

Additional Film Notes

The Clockmaker (L'Horloger de Saint Paul)
1974 (105 min.)

The Simenon Inspiration and Divergences: The film was inspired by a 1954 Simenon novel, *The Watchmaker of Everton*, set in America in the 1930s, about immigrants who were not completely at home in their new society. Tavernier found that Simenon's world contained "very pointed and strong images that harbor a specific emotion," and he cites as examples the scene where the police officer says to a normal man in the early hours of the morning: "Your son killed a man." When the man returns home he goes to bed and tries to picture this son. There is also the scene when, after visiting his son in prison, the father leaves with a strange feeling of happiness (Bonneville 1982, 28). The story also interested Tavernier because "there is the unexpected discovery of a drama in the life of someone who is completely average" (Hurley 1982, 166).

In a 1974 interview, Tavernier noted that what had immediately grabbed his attention in the novel was the simple statement made during the trial: "I stand behind my son," which gave Tavernier the desire to do a film dealing with the love of father for son (Braucourt 1974, 63). Tavernier himself took custody of his children for a while when he and his wife Colo separated, and he, like Michel Descombes, was a single father (Coursodon 1986, 23). In a 1986 interview, he commented that he had "recently come to realize the importance of families in [his] work. I do not seem to be able to make a film without a family in it—or else it is the *lack* of a family, of family ties, that plays a major role" (Coursodon 1986, 22).

Critic Guy Braucourt noted that the film evokes Roger Martin du Gard's comment: "When I meet two men, one older and the other young, who walk side by side without finding anything to say to one another, I know it is a father and his son" (Braucourt 1974, 62). Tavernier was to experience just such an estrangement a decade later when his own son Nils became a drug addict. He confronted that problem cinematically only after Nils had recovered.

The Child's Look: From within a moving train, a child's uncomprehending stare directed at a car on fire opens the film. We realize later that this was the car the son blew up. The initial scene prepares us for a violence for which the father himself was unprepared.

Epiphanic Moments in *The Clockmaker*: The discovery of the father's and son's common bond in revolt against the scum on top brings about the brief epiphanic moment, denoted by the brief smile on the father's face as he walks away after the prison visit. Simenon places this epiphanic moment early in the story, when the father is lying on his son's bed after hearing of the murder. Tavernier's placement of it at the end, after a real conversation with his son where he discovers the possibility of communing with his son, is more convincing. Simenon's analysis, however, is perfectly applicable: he "felt the mingling of his own life and that of the universe, his heart beating with the same rhythm as the earth, as the grass which surrounded him, as the leaves of the trees which rustled above his head" (B.B., D.R.-B. 1992, 56-57). As Descombes leaves the prison, the sounds of traffic give way to singing birds and then stringed instruments. The way in which Descombes crosses the street, oblivious to anyone else on it, as well as the brief smile, communicates the feeling of that epiphany to the spectator and ends the otherwise grim film on an upbeat note.

Clean Slate (*Coup de Torchon*)
1981 (128 min.)

Source: The plot was inspired by *Pop. 1280*, a novel by an American writer, Jim Thompson (d. 1977), set in the South. A southern village sheriff is on a brutal campaign to clean up the human trash in his district. Originally published in paperback in 1963, translated into French in 1966, it was the one-thousandth title in the famous *Série Noire* thriller collection of the Gallimard publishing house. Though Thompson is little known in the United States, he is highly esteemed in France, where his admirers are not afraid to draw comparisons between him and literary giants like Henry Miller and Céline.

Concepts Found in the Novel: Tavernier and joint script-writer Jean Aurenche (the then eighty-two-year-old *doyen* of French scriptwriters) gave it considerable more depth. Tavernier had the idea of transposing the story to French Africa, thereby making it impossible for French spectators to say racial prejudice is just an American problem, not theirs.

In Thompson's novel there was already present the character of whom Tavernier would say, "you do not know if the character says what he says to excuse what he has just done or if he does things as a consequence of what he has just said. You never know. And I do not know if the character himself knows." As a consequence, when directing Noiret, he told him that he did not even want Noiret to be sure why he did or said something. A statement that he took directly from Thompson and put in the mouth of Cordier is, "Where is good, where is evil" ["Où est le bien, où est le mal"]. Tavernier suggested to Aurenche the scene in the cinema, with Huguette, Rose and Nono watching the film from behind the screen and perceiving the silhouettes of Cordier and Anne, the schoolteacher. The scene permits Cordier to cuddle up with Anne (he falls asleep on her shoulder), his wife Huguette and his mistress Rose as witnesses. Aurenche added the storm to bring Cordier and the schoolteacher even closer together. The whole sequence is a unique use of film within film, film incorporated into plot. Structurally it permits Cordier to appear to treat Huguette as Huguette treats him—as object, but he does it accidentally.

Color Details: Tavernier did not want the post-card quality of many films shot in Africa. As a consequence, certain colors were eliminated. A train was repainted just so the color would blend better with the background. Anything that suggested the exotic was eliminated. The usual wild animals of African films are curiously absent (Cèbe 1981, 30).

Esthetic Unity: The film ends with the reverse of the opening scene, with differences. It begins with Cordier watching young African boys eating ants just before an eclipse of the sun; it ends with the same contemplation, no eclipse, and a revolver in hand. But the spectator is quite uncertain as to the meaning of the revolver now. There is no neat, pat, comfortable conclusion, yet esthetically, the film is complete, though questioning.

A Sunday in the Country (Un Dimanche à la Campagne) 1984 (94 min.)

Based on a short novel by Pierre Bost, *Monsieur Ladmiral va bientôt mourir* (1945), the scenario was completed in two months and the shooting took only thirty-three days. Tavernier attributes this rapidity to the preparation for the subject he had from just recently doing a documentary of the aged Philippe Soupault. And he had used Jean Aurenche and Pierre Bost, both in their seventies at the time, to do the screenplay for his first film, *The Clockmaker* (1973). (Bost died in 1975.)

Louis Ducreux at the age of seventy-three had had a long career in the theater but had never been in a film before. The painting he is supposed to have painted when he was young is from his private collection. In addition to acting in, staging, and adapting plays, Ducreux wrote several popular songs, including the theme song for Max Ophul's *La Ronde* (1950). One of his compositions, a polka, is the music for Ladmiral's last dance with his daughter.

Music as the Rhythm and Motion: Listening to Gabriel Fauré's later quintets gave Tavernier ideas for certain scenes, such as the return from the train station (Fauré's Piano and String Quintet, opus 115; Piano and String Trio, opus 120; String Quartet, opus 121).

Differences Between Book and Film: The conversation regarding his "missed" art is a voice-over in the novel instead of a conversation, held with his daughter, an encounter between father and daughter that never occurs in the novel. In the novel, the father never returns to his canvas or his painting. The novel ends merely with the comment of the father to an acquaintance who asks him the next day if family had visited him over the weekend. "Yes, my daughter." There is no mention of his son's family.

Tavernier also added flashbacks and flash-forwards that were not in the book, each member of the family having one, giving a greater depth and feeling to the family gathering. Not only do images of the deceased Madame Ladmiral occur, but Irene reads in Mireille's palm that she will die and the son imagines his father's death.

'Round Midnight
1986 (131 min.)

The story of Dale Turner succeeds in doing what no other film made about jazz has yet done. It takes jazz seriously as a musical form and does not cheat on the musical integrity for the sake of a plot. Dexter Gordon plays a saxophonist, not a pianist, and is a composite of Lester Young and Bud Powell. Instead of a pianist, Tavernier looked for a tenor saxophonist because for him, it is the quintessential instrument of bebop. Gordon himself shared in the development of bebop style in the 1960s (whereas the film is supposedly set in the late 1950s) and wandered in Europe for several years. He communicates his own aura, above all, but one that is a jazz musician, and not a Hollywood character acting like one. All critics agree that a professional actor (at age sixty-three, this was Gordon's first role) would not have been as convincing.

Martin Scorcese himself plays Goodley, Dale's villainous manager, and another director, John Berry, plays the nightclub manager, Ben. The cast is not short of great jazz musicians turned actors. Herbie Hancock not only composed, arranged, and conducted the music, for which he won an Oscar, but the music itself was recorded live, on the set, and not in a sound studio.

Beatrice (*La Passion Béatrice*)
1987 (131 min.)

Principal Characters: Julie Delpy plays the daughter, Beatrice. By selling off property to pay the ransom for the return of her father and brother, she demonstrates her devotion to a father who departed when she was too young to know him, yet for whom she now yearns.

Tavernier felt female characters in cinema were being treated with regrettable Puritan "moralism." Though "horrendous and immoral things happen to Beatrice, she never becomes a female object, but remains a tragic individual. The word *passion* is utilized in two ways: the passion of a girl for the love of all she might do and passion in the sense of suffering" (Coulombe and Wera 1988, 12). Honest, if proud, she never plays to the spectator's sympathy, never seeks pity for her situation. Tavernier selected Julie Delpy for the role because of her *regard*, the way she looks at someone. Indeed, there is nothing supplicating in her look, but rather a directness that questions the social structure to which she is subjected. Her white horse is an almost blatant symbol of her innocence and purity.

Bernard-Pierre Donnadieu juggles the delicate role of François de Cortemare, at once monstrous and pitiable. Taken prisoner by the English, he returns with his son (whom he publicly humiliates), thanks to the ransom paid by his daughter. Cortemare commits horrors, according to Tavernier, in hopes of provoking the all-powerful God to act, in order to find proof of his existence. As disgusted with his sins as we are, he remains in one of the peasant huts he has set afire to die for his sins. He does not reject God, but rather struggles with him according to a Celtic tradition that Colo knew well.

Setting: A refurbished Cathare castle in the southwest of France, in the province of Aude, the Château de Puivert near Carcassonne was used as the set for the fourteenth-century action occurring during the Hundred Years' War. The reconstruction of this historical period was not without challenges. The logistics of dealing with a bunch of horsemen, children underfoot, cattle and other animals as well as the horses are formidable. Tavernier tells us that during the burning of the village the firemen announced that there was not enough water and that the fire threatened to spread.

Life and Nothing But (La Vie et Rien d'Autre...) *1989* (130 min.)

It was Philippe Noiret's seventh film made with Tavernier (his own hundredth film). Sabine Azéma, as Irène de Courtil, played the part of another Irene in Tavernier's *Sunday in the Country*. Situated in 1920, the film was shot in Meuse and in the Haute-Marne. The tunnel scenes were shot seventy kilometers from Saint-Didier. The ceremony selecting the unknown soldier was shot in a subterranean citadel of Verdun where it actually took place (Laurendeau 1989, 44).

Daddy Nostalgia
1990 (106 min.)

Colo Tavernier O'Hagen's autobiographical script is based on her Irish family up-bringing.

Like *Sunday in the Country* and *The Clockmaker*, *Daddy Nostalgia* deals with the generation gap, in this case between father and daughter. The social convention that prevented communication is the right of the successful male to enjoy the pleasures of life, his family duties being satisfied as long as he provides the economic wherewithall for their survival. The film questions this male egocentric position. Because of the techniques Tavernier uses, the story does not become in the least sentimentalized. The spectator feels the aches society has fostered in families, but there are no tears in the movie.

Dirk Bogarde, age seventy, plays the English father in his first performance since Fassbinder's *Despair* (1978). He manages a delicate balancing act between the gallant illusion he wants to leave, even though he is in intense pain and suffering. After a successful career in British films, Bogarde moved to a Provençal farmhouse to write for a while, lending part of his own autobiography to the plot.

Odette Laure, as the wife, is, according to Dick Bogarde, "best known in France as a musical lady who used to sing mildly risqué songs [and] refuses to speak English, so we improvised a line around that fact" (Billington 1991, 13).

L.627 (L.627)
1992 (145 min.)

The title, *L.627*, is the article of the French legal code intended to repress violations related to the possession, traffic, and consummation of drugs.

Nils Tavernier, the director's son, began taking drugs at the age of twelve (1980), escaping in 1985 after an attempted suicide (Fitoussi 1992, 38). He was twenty-six years of age in 1992 when Tavernier shot the film with Nils' participation both as actor and scriptwriter. The film chronicles the struggle against drug-trafficking that confronts the ordinary law enforcement officer (no Rambo) dedicated to that task.

Filmography:
Bertrand Tavernier as Director

"Une Chance explosive" — 1964 (24 min. episode of *La Chance et L'Amour*)

Producer:	Georges de Beauregard
Screenplay:	Bertrand Tavernier
	Nicolas Vogel
Photography:	Alain Levent
Music:	Antoine Duhamel
Editing:	Armand Psenny
Cast:	
Alain Lorriere	Michel Auclair
Camilly	Bertrand Blier
Sophie	Iran Eory

"Le Baiser de Judas" — 1964 (14 min. episode of *Les Baisers*)

Producer:	Georges de Beauregard
Screenplay:	Bertrand Tavernier
	Claude-Jean Philippe
	Roger Tailleur
Photography:	Raoul Coutard
Music:	Eddie Vartan
Editing:	Etiennette Muse
Cast:	
Tiffany	Laetitia Roman
Sylvie	Judy Del Carril
Robert	Bernard Rousselet

The Clockmaker (*L'Horloger de Saint Paul*) — 1974 (105 min.)

Producer:	Raymond Danon
Screenplay:	Jean Aurenche
	Pierre Bost
	Bertrand Tavernier

(Based on a novel by Georges Simenon, *L'Horloger d'Everton*)

Photography:	Pierre-William Glenn
Design:	Jean Mandaroux
Music:	Philippe Sarde
Editing:	Armand Psenny
Cast:	
Michel Descombes	Philippe Noiret
Commissaire Guiboud	Jean Rochefort
Antoine	Jacques Denis
Bernard Descombes	Sylvain Rougerie
Liliane Torini	Christine Pascal
Madeleine Fourmet	Andrée Tainsy
The little girl in the train	Tiffany Tavernier

Awards: Silver Bear Special Jury Prize 1974

Let Joy Reign Supreme (*Que la Fête commence*) — 1975 (120 min.)

Producer:	Michelle de Broca
Screenplay:	Jean Aurenche
	Bertrand Tavernier

(Based on the novel by Alexandre Dumas, *La Fille du Régent*)

Photography:	Pierre-William Glenn
Design:	Pierre Guffroy
Music:	Philippe Sarde
	Philippe D'Orléans
Editing:	Armand Psenny
Cast:	
Philippe D'Orleans	Philippe Noiret
Abbé	Jean Rochefort
Marquis Pontcallec	Jean-Pierre Marielle
Emilie	Christine Pascal
Mme. Parabere de Bourbon	Marina Vlady
Duc De Bourbon	Gerard Desarthe

Awards: Césars for Best Director, Best Supporting Actor, and Best
Supporting Actress, and Best Writing 1974

The Judge and the Assassin *(Le Juge et l'Assassin)* — 1975 (130 min.)

Producer:	Raymond Danon
Screenplay:	Bertrand Tavernier
	Jean Aurenche
	Pierre Bost
Photography:	Pierre-William Glenn
Design:	Antoine Roman
Music:	Philippe Sarde
Editing:	Armand Psenny
Cast:	
Judge Rousseau	Philippe Noiret
Sgt. Joseph Bouvier	Michel Galabru
Rose	Isabelle Huppert
Villedieu	Jean-Claude Brialy
Mme. Rousseau	Renée Faure
Louise Lesueur	Cecile Vassort

Awards: Césars Best Actor, Best Writing 1977

Spoiled Children *(Les Enfants Gâtés)* — 1977 (113 min.)

Producer:	Alain Sarde
Screenplay:	Christine Pascal
	Charlotte Dubreuil
	Bertrand Tavernier
Photography:	Alain Levant
Music:	Philippe Sarde
Editing:	Armand Psenny
Cast:	
Bernard	Michel Piccoli
Anne	Christine Pascal
Pierre	Michel Aumont
Marcel	Gerard Jugnot
Catherine	Arlette Bonnard
Mouchot	Georges Riquier
Patrice	Gerard Zimmerman

Dedication: "toute caresse, toute confiance se survivent. Paul Eluard à Colo, parceque c'est normal..."

Deathwatch *(La Mort en Direct)* — 1980 (128 min.)
Producer: Gabriel Boustiani
                             Bertrand Tavernier
Screenplay: David Rayfiel
                             Bertrand Tavernier
(Adaption of David Compton, *The Continuous Katherine Mortenhoe)*
Photography: Pierre-William Glenn
Design: Tony Pratt
Music: Antoine Duhamel
Editing: Armand Psenny
Cast:
  Katherine Mortenhoe   Romy Schneider
  Roddy   Harvey Keitel
  Vincent Ferriman   Harry Dean Stanton
  Tracey   Therese Liotard
  Gerald Mortenhoe   Max Von Sydow
Cost: $3,000,000

A Week's Vacation *(Une Semaine de Vacances)* — May 1980 (102 min.)
Producer: Alain Sarde
Screenplay: Colo Tavernier
                             Bertrand Tavernier
                             Marie-Françoise Hans
Photography: Pierre-William Glenn
Design: Baptiste Poirot
Music: Pierre Papadiamandis
Editing: Armand Psenny
                             Sophie Cornu
Cast:
  Laurence   Nathalie Baye
  Pierre   Gerard Lanvin
  Mancheron   Michel Galabru
  Descombes   Philippe Noiret
  Sabouret   Philippe Leotard
  Anne   Flore Fitzgerald
  Father   Jean Daste
  Mother   Marie-Louise Ebeli
Cost: $800,000; Shooting time: 6 weeks

Clean Slate (Coup de Torchon) — 1981 (128 min.)
Producer: Adolphe Viezzi
                              Henri Lassa
Screenplay: Bertrand Tavernier
                              Jean Aurenche
(Based on the novel by Jim Thompson, *Pop. 1280)*
Photography: Pierre-William Glenn
Design: Alexandre Trauner
Music: Philippe Sarde
Editing: Armand Psenny
Cast:
  Lucien Cordier   Philippe Noiret
  Rose   Isabelle Huppert
  Le Peron/his brother   Jean-Pierre Marielle
  Huguette   Stéphane Audran
  Nono   Eddy Mitchell
  Chavasson   Guy Marchand
  Anne   Irene Skobline
  Vanderbrouck   Michel Beaune

Philippe Soupault ou le surréalisme — 1982 (156 min.) (doc.)
Producer: Danièle Delorme
Screenplay: Bertrand Tavernier
                              Jean Aurenche
Photography: Jean-François Gondre
Music: Erik Satie
                              Sidney Bechet
                              Lester Young
                              Archie Schepp
Editing: Luce Grünenwaldt

Mississippi Blues — 1984 (101 minutes) (co-director)

Co-Directors:	Bertrand Tavernier
	Robert Parrish
Producers:	Bertrand Tavernier
	Yannick Bernard
Screenplay:	Bertrand Tavernier
	Robert Parrish
Cameraman:	Pierre-William Glenn
Editors:	Ariane Boeglin
	Agnes Vaurigaud

Note: *October Country* was the televised version of *Mississippi Blues*

A Sunday in the Country (*Un Dimanche à la Campagne*) — 1984 (94 min.)

Producer:	Alain Sarde
Screenplay:	Bertrand Tavernier
	Colo Tavernier

(Adaption of Pierre Bost, *Monsieur Ladmiral va bientôt mourir*)

Photography:	Bruno de Keyzer
Design:	Patrice Mercier
Music:	Gabriel Fauré
Editing:	Armand Psenny
Cast:	
Mr. Ladmiral	Louis Ducreux
Irene	Sabine Azéma
Gonzague	Michel Aumont
Marie-Thérèse	Geneviève Mnich
Mercédès	Monique Chaumette
Mme. Ladmiral	Claude Winter

Shooting time: 33 days

Awards: Cannes Film Festival Best Director 1984; Césars Best Actress (Azéma), Best Cinematography, Best Writing 1985; New York Film Critics Award Best Foreign Film 1984

'Round Midnight (*Autour de Minuit*) — 1986 (131 min.)

Producer:	Irwin Winkler
Screenplay:	Bertrand Tavernier
	David Rayfiel
Photography:	Bruno de Keyzer
Design:	Alexandre Trauner
Editor:	Armand Psenny
Music:	Herbie Hancock, composer and conductor

Cast:

Dale Turner	Dexter Gordon
Francis Borier	François Cluzet
Bérangère	Gabrielle Haker
Buttercup	Sandra Reaves-Phillips
Darcey Leigh	Lonette McKee
Sylvie	Christine Pascal
Eddie Wayne	Herbie Hancock
Ace	Bobby Hutcherson
Mr. Borier	Pierre Trabaud
Mrs. Borier	Frédérique Meininger
Ben	John Berry
Goodley	Martin Scorsese

Also with: Ron Carter, Billy Higgins, Freddie Hubbard, John McLaughlin, Eric Le Lann, Pierre Michelot, Palle Mikkelborg, Mads Vinding, Wayne Shorter, Cedar Walton, Tony Williams, Liliane Rovère, Ged Marlon, Hart Leroy Bibbs, Benoit Regent, Victoria Gabrielle Platt, Arthur French, Alain Sarde, Philippe Noiret, Eddy Mitchell.

Cost: $3 million

Awards: Los Angeles Film Critics Association Award Best Music 1986; Academy Award Best Original Score 1987; Césars Best Music and Best Sound 1987; Bodil Award Best European Film 1988

Béatrice (*La Passion Béatrice*) — 1987 (131 min.)
Producer: Adolphe Viezzi
Screenplay: Colo Tavernier O'Hagan
Photography: Bruno de Keyzer
Design: Guy-Claude François
Music: Ron Carter
Editing: Armand Psenny
Cast:
 François de Cortemare   Bernard-Pierre Donnadieu
 Béatrice   Julie Delpy
 Arnaud   Nils Tavernier
 Mother François   Monique Chaumette
 Hélène   Michèle Gleizer
 Richard   Maxime Leroux
 Raoul   Robert Dhery
 The Priest   Claude Duneton
 Bertrand Lemartin   Jean-Claude Adelin
 Recluse   Albane Guilhe
 Jehan   Jean-Luc Rivals
Award: César Best Costume Design 1988

Lyon, Le Regard Intérieur — 1988 (57 min.) (doc. for TV)
Screenplay: Bertrand Tavernier
Photography: Alain Choquart
Editing: Armand Psenny

Life and Nothing But (*La Vie et Rien d'Autre*) — 1989 (130 min.)

Producer:	René Cleitman
Assistant Director:	Tristan Ganne
Screenplay:	Jean Cosmos
	Bertrand Tavernier
Photography:	Bruno de Keyzer
Design:	Guy-Claude François
Music:	Oswald d'Andrea
Editing:	Armand Psenny
Cast:	
Dellaplane	Philippe Noiret
Irène	Sabine Azéma
Alice	Pascal Vignal
Mercadot	Maurice Barrier
Perrin	François Perrot
André	Jean Pol Dubois
Lieutenant Trévisse	Daniel Russo
Général Villerieux	Michel Duchossoy

Cost: $4.3 million; Shooting time: 8 weeks

Awards: British Academy Award Best Foreign Film 1989; European Film Special Prize of the Jury 1989; Tokyo International Film Festival Best Artistic Contribution 1989; Césars Best Actor (Noiret), Best Score 1990; Los Angeles Film Critics Association Award Best Foreign Film 1990

Daddy Nostalgia (*Daddy Nostalgie*) — 1990 (106 Min.)

Producer:	Adolphe Viezzi
Screenplay:	Colo Tavernier O'Hagan
Photography:	Denis Lenoir
Design:	Robert LeCorre
Music:	Antoine Duhamel
Editing:	Ariane Boeglin
Cast:	
Daddy	Dirk Bogarde
Caroline	Jane Birkin
Miche	Odette Laure
Juliette	Emmanuelle Bataille
Barbara	Charlotte Kady
Old Man in Métro	Louis Ducreux

The Undeclared War (*La Guerre sans nom*) — 1991 (235 min.)
    Producer: Jean-Pierre Guérin
    Screenplay: Patrick Rotman
                              Bertrand Tavernier
    Photography: Alain Choquart
    Editing: Luce Grünenwaldt
    Award: Bergamo Film Special Mention 1992

L.627 — 1992 (145 min.)
    Producer: Alain Sarde
                              Frederic Bourboulon
    Screenplay: Michèle Alexandre
                              Bertrand Tavernier
    Photography: Alain Choquart
    Design: Guy-Claude François
    Music: Philippe Sarde
    Editing: Ariane Boeglin
    Cast:
      Lucien "Lulu" Marguet   Didier Bezace
      Dominique "Dodo" Cantoni   Jean-Paul Comart
      Marie   Charlotte Kady
      Manuel   Jean-Roger Milo
      Vincent   Nils Tavernier
      Antoine   Philippe Torreton
      Cécile   Lara Guirao
      Kathy   Cécile Garcia-Fogel
      Adoré   Claude Brosset
    Dedication: to Nils Tavernier

The Daughter of D'Artagnan (*La Fille de D'Artagnan*) — 1994
(125 min.)

Producer:	Frederic Bourboulon
Screenplay:	Michel Leviant
	Bertrand Tavernier
	Jean Cosmos

(Based on an idea by Riccardo Freda, Eric Poindron)

Photography:	Patrick Blossiner
Music:	Philippe Sarde
Editing:	Ariane Boeglin
Cast:	
Eloise	Sophie Marceau
Quentin	Nils Tavernier
D'Artagnan	Philippe Noiret
Athos	Jean-Luc Bideau
Porthos	Raoul Billerey
Aramis	Sami Frey
Lady in Red	Charlotte Kady
Mazarin	Luigi Proietti
Duke of Crassac	Claude Rich
Planchet	Jean-Paul Roussillon

Fresh Bait (*L'Appât*) — 1995 (117 min.)
> Producers: René Cleitman
>   Frederic Bourboulon
> Screenplay: Colo Tavernier O'Hagan
>   Bertrand Tavernier
> (Based on the book by Morgan Sportès)
> Photography: Alain Choquart
> Design: Emile Ghico
> Music: Philippe Haim
> Editing: Luce Grunenwaldt
> Cast:
>   Nathalie   Marie Gillain
>   Eric   Olivier Sitruk
>   Bruno   Bruno Putzulu
>   Alain   Richard Berry
>   Antoine   Philippe Duclos
>   Karine   Marie Ravel
>   Patricia   Clothilde Courau
> Award: Berlin International Film Festival Golden Bear Award 1995

Captain Conan (*Capitaine Conan*) — 1996 (129 min.)
> Producer: Alain Sarde
>   Frederic Bourboulon
> Screenplay: Jean Cosmos
>   Bertrand Tavernier
> (Based on a 1934 autobiographical novel by Roger Vercel)
> Photography: Alain Choquart
> Design: Guy-Claude Françoise
> Music: Oswald D'Andréa
> Editing: Luce Grunenwaldt
> Cast:
>   Conan   Philippe Torreton
>   Norbert   Samuel Le Bihan
>   Lt. De Scève   Bernard Le Coq
>   Madeleine Erlane   Catherine Rich
>   Commandant Bouvier   François Berléand
>   Gen. Pitard de Lauzier Claude Rich
> Awards: San Sebastian Silver Seashell Best Production Design 1996;
>   Césars Best Director and Best Actor (Torreton) 1997

Bibliography

Ansen, David. "Lady Sweets Sings the Blues." *Newsweek* (Oct. 20, 1986): 78.

———. "An Executioner's Song." *Newsweek* (Jan. 3, 1983): 53-54.

Arecco, Sergio. *Bertrand Tavernier*. Florence, Italy: Il Castoro, 1993.

Audé, Françoise and Hubert Niogret. "Après trente ans de silence." *Positif* 374 (Apr. 1992): 26-31.

Audé, Françoise, Jean-Pierre Jeancolas and Paul Louis Thirard. "Entretien avec Bertrand Tavernier." *Positif* 227 (Feb. 1980): 57-64.

B.B. and D.R.-B. "Bertrand Tavernier: Une histoire d'ambiguïtés." *La Revue du cinéma* 485 (Sept. 1992b): 59-60.

———. "Entretien avec Bertrand Tavernier: le réalisme en question." *La Revue du cinéma* 485 (Sept. 1992a): 55-58.

Baecque, Antoine de and Thierry Jousse. "Autour de Bertrand Tavernier." *Cahiers du cinéma* 478 (1994): 44-49.

Bates, Robin. "Holes in the Sausage of History: May '68 as Absent Center in Three European Films." *Cinema Journal* 24, 3 (Spring 1985): 24-42.

Bazin, André, Jacques Becker, Charles Bitsch, Claude Chabrol, Michel Delahaye, Jean Domarchi, Jacques Doniol-Valcroze, Jean Douchet, Jean-Luc Godard, Fereydoun Hoveyda, Jacques Rivette, Eric Rohmer, Maurice Schérer, and François Truffaut. *La Politique des Auteurs*. Paris: Editions Champ Libre, 1972.

Benoit, Claude. "Bertrand Tavernier: *Des Enfants gâtés.*" *Jeune Cinéma* 105 (Sept.-Oct. 1977): 20-25.

———. "Bertrand Tavernier: par delà Simenon, un univers personnel." *Jeune cinéma* 77 (Mar. 1974): 5-13.

Benson, Edward. "'The Clockmaker': A Tale of Two Cultures." *Film Criticism* 6, 1 (1981): 55-62.

Bertin-Maghit, Jean-Pierre. "Trois cinéastes en quête de l'histoire." *Positif* 227 (Feb. 1980): 57-64.

———. "Trois cinéastes en quête de l'histoire." *La Revue du cinéma* 352 (July-Aug. 1980): 108-17.

Beylie, Claude. "Entretien avec Bertrand Tavernier." *Ecran* (April 15, 1976): 51-52.

Billington, Michael. "Dirk Bogarde Journeys Into 'Nostalgia'." *New York Times* (Apr. 7, 1991): 13, 16.

Bion, Danièle. *Bertrand Tavernier: cinéaste de l'émotion.* Paris: Hatier, 1984.

Blanchot, Maurice. "Français, Encore un Effort..." *La Nouvelle revue française* 154 (Oct. 1965): 600-618.

Bonneville, Léo. "Bertrand Tavernier: A propos de *L.627.*" *Sequences* 163 (Mar. 1993): 14-16.

———. "Rencontre avec Bertrand Tavernier." *Sequences* 110 (Oct. 1982): 24-36.

Braucourt, Guy. "*L'Horloger de Saint-Paul.*" *Ecran* 21 (Jan. 1974): 62-64.

Cardullo, B. "The Wake of War." *Hudson Review* 44 (1991): 475-84.

Cèbe, Gilles. "Bertrand Tavernier." *Cinématographe* 71 (Oct. 1981): 27-30.

———. "Bertrand Tavernier après quatre films." *Ecran* 62 (Sept. 1977): 34-40.

———. "Entretien avec Bertrand Tavernier." *Revue du Cinéma* 337 (June 1980a): 20-22.

———. "Tavernier en direct (Entretien)." *La Revue du Cinéma* 346 (Jan. 1980b): 25-28.

Ciment, Michel. "Sunday in the Country with Bertrand." *American Film* 10 (Oct. 1984): 30-35.

Ciment, Michel, Jean-Pierre Jeancolas, Isabelle Jordan, and Paul Louis Thirard. "Entretien avec Bertrand Tavernier." *Positif* 279 (May 1984): 5-14.

Coulombe, Michel and Françoise Wera. "Entretien avec Bertrand Tavernier." *Cinébulles* VII, 4 (May-July 1988): 12-15.

Coursodon, Jean-Pierre. "Round Midnight: An Interview with Bertrand Tavernier." *Cineaste* 15, 2 (1986): 18-23.

Coursodon, Jean Pierre and Bertrand Tavernier. *Cinquante ans de cinéma américain*. Paris: Nathan, 1991.

Cros, Jean-Louis. "Fuller au Crible, Table ronde avec: Jacqueline Lajeunesse, Marcel Martin. Daniel Serceau, Noel Simsolo, Bertrand Tavernier, and Jacques Zimmer." *Revue du Cinéma* 360 (April 1981): 81-89.

Damisch, Hubert. "L'écriture sans mesures." *Tel Quel* 28 (1967): 51-65.

Demeure, Jacques and Paul-Louis Thirard. "Entretien avec Bertrand Tavernier." *Positif* 156 (Feb. 1974): 41-48.

Dempsey, Michael. "All the Colors: Bertrand Tavernier Talks about *Round Midnight*." *Film Quarterly* 40, 3 (1987): 2-11.

Douin, Jean-Luc. *Tavernier*. Paris: Edilig, 1988.

Fitoussi, Michèle. "Bertrand Tavernier: un père contre la drogue." *Elle* 2436 (Sept. 7, 1992): 35-40.

Forbes, Jill. *The Cinema in France After the New Wave*. London: Macmillan, 1992, 153-70.

Foucault, Michel. *The Order of Things; an Archeology of the Human Sciences*. New York: Vintage Books, 1970. (Translation of *Les mots et les choses; une archéologie des sciences humaines*, Paris: Gallimard, 1966.)

Freud, Sigmund. "Instincts and Their Vicissitudes." *The Major Works of Sigmund Freud* (Chicago: Encyclopaedia Britannica, Inc., 1952): 412-421.

Garrity, Henry A. "Camera as Meaning in *Coup de Torchon*." *Studies in the Humanities* 11 (1984): 56-60.

Gilliatt, Penelope. "Wild Justice." *New Yorker* (Aug. 9, 1976): 49-52.

Gillissen, Olivier, Danièle Parra, and Christian Bosséno. "Un Cinéaste inclassable: Bertrand Tavernier." *La Revue du cinéma* 393 (April 1984): 55-64.

Gow, Gordon. "The Clockmaker of Saint-Paul." *Films and Filming* 20 (June 1974): 50-51.

Groult, Roland. "Bertrand Tavernier." *Sequences* 133 (March 1988): 33-35.

Hackman, William. "A Parisian in America." *Film Comment* 22 (Sept.-Oct. 1986): 23-26.

Hennebelle, Guy and Monique Hennebelle. "Vers un nouveau réalisme: Le Cinéma de Bertrand Tavernier." *Ecran* 61-62 (Sept. 1977): 19-32; (Oct. 15, 1977): 23-33.

Hoffman, Eva. "After the New Wave, Tavernier." *New York Times* 135, sec. 6 (Dec. 8, 1985): 96-109.

Hurley, Joseph. "Tavernier et Noiret: An Interview with France's Unique Director-Actor Collaboration." *Films in Review* 34 (March 1982): 163-70.

———. "Tavernier et Noiret Encore." *Films in Review* 34 (April 1983): 230-37.

Jacobowitz, Florence, Richard Lippe, and Robin Wood. "The Survival of Mise-en-scène: An Interview with Bertrand Tavernier." *CineAction!* (Dec. 1986): 65-73.

Jaehne, Karen. "La Guerre n'est pas finie: An Interview with Bertrand Tavernier and Philippe Noiret." *Cineaste* 18, 1 (1990): 9-13.

"Le Juge et l'assassin." *Revue du Cinéma* 331 bis (1978): 119-28.

Kauffman, Stuart A. *The Origins of Order: Self-Organization and Selection in Evolution.* New York: Oxford University Press, 1993.

Kauffmann, Stanley. "The Judge and the Assassin." *New Republic* 187 (Sept. 6, 1982): 24-26.

Kemp, P. "Tavernier on Mackendrick." *Sight and Sound* 4 (Aug. 1994): 16-20.

Kroll, Jack. "A Radical Bourgeois." *Newsweek* (Aug. 30, 1976): 74.

Laurendeau, Francine. "Interview: Bertrand Tavernier." *Sequences* 143 (Nov. 1989): 41-46.

Le Morvan, Gilles. "La Recherche du sang perdu." *L'Humanité* (Sept. 6, 1989): 25.

Lequeux, Michel. "La Passion Béatrice." *Grand Angle* 15, 102 (Feb. 1988): 21-24.

Magretta, W.-R. and J. Magretta. "'The Clockmaker': From Novel to Film." *Literature/Film Quarterly* 7, 4 (1979): 277-84.

Maillet, Dominique. "Bertrand Tavernier." *Cinématographe* 100 (May 1984): 34-36.

Mandel, Howard. "Round Midnight." *Down Beat* (Jan. 1987): 22-23.

McGilligan, Patrick. "Journey into Light." *Film Comment* 28, 2 (Mar.-Apr. 1992): 6-19.

Milne, Tom. "Horloger de St. Paul, L'." *Monthly Film Bulletin* 44, 521 (June 1977): 123.

Paletz, Gabriel M. *"Daddy Nostalgia."* *Film Quarterly* 45 (1992): 45-49.

Quart, Leonard and Lenny Rubenstein. "Blending the Personal with the Political: An Interview with Bertrand Tavernier." *Cineaste* 8 (1978): 25-27, 55.

Rabourdin, Dominique. "Entretien avec Bertrand Tavernier." *Cinéma* 75, 198 (May 1975): 70-79.

Sade, Alphonse, Marquis de. *Justine*. Paris: Union Générale d'Éditions, 1969.

Simenon, Georges. *The Watchmaker of Everton*, tr. Norman Denny. London: White Lion Publishers Ltd., 1975.

Stewart, Garrett. "Death Watch." *Film Quarterly* 37 (1983): 16-22.

Tavernier, Bertrand. "20 Questions aux cinéastes." *Cahiers du Cinéma* 323 (May 1981): 72-73.

———. *Les Amis Américains*. Lyons: Institute Lumière / Actes Sud, 1993.

———. *La Guerre sans Nom: les appelés d'Algérie*. Paris: Le Seuil, 1992.

———. "L'Horloger de Saint-Paul: découpage et dialogues in extenso." *Avant-Scène du Cinéma* 147 (May 1974): 8-40.

———. "Une Lettre de Bertrand Tavernier." *Cahiers du cinéma* 332 (Feb. 1982): xii-xiii.

———. "Michael Powell, une vie au cinema." *Positif* 351 (May 1990): 54-58.

———. "Notes Eparses." *Positif* 200-202 (Dec. 1977-Jan. 78): 206-10.

———. Preface to Parrish, Robert. *J'ai grandi à Hollywood*. Paris: Stock, 1980.

———. *Qu'est'ce qu'on attend?* Paris: Ed. du Seuil, 1993.

Tavernier, Bertrand and Jean Cosmos. "La Vie et Rien d'Autre: Découpage plan à plan après montage." *Avant-Scène du Cinéma* 388 (January 1990): 13-120.

Tavernier, Bertrand and Jean Pierre Coursodon. *See* Coursodon.

Westerbeck, Colin L., Jr. "African Meltdown: Mad Dogs and Frenchmen." *Commonweal* 86 (Feb. 11, 1983): 86-87.

Wood, Robin. "Tavernier, Bertrand." *International Dictionary of Films and Filmmakers - 2: Directors*. Detroit: St. James Press, 1990: 833-34.

Yakir, Dan. "Painting Pictures." *Film Comment* 20 (Sept. 1984): 18-22.

Zants, Emily. *Creative Encounters with French Film*. Lewiston, N.Y.: Edwin Mellen Press, 1993.

———. *Chaos Theory, Complexity, Cinema and the Evolution of the French Novel*. Lewiston, N.Y.: Edwin Mellen Press, 1996.

Zarader, Jean-Pierre. "Le mal et son pardon dans l'oeuvre cinématographique de Bertrand Tavernier." *Revue de métaphysique et de morale* 90, 2 (April-June 1985): 247-64.

Index

About the Author

Emily Zants became interested in French film in the mid 1980s as a way to teach participatory enjoyment of literature as well as the other arts, considering that Hollywood and American television only show today's youth a passive entertainment mode of pleasure. She published a text, *Creative Encounters with French Films*, to assist her in that enterprise.

Having specialized in the novel—her dissertation done at Columbia University explored the *Aesthetics of the New Novel in France*—she wrote numerous articles dealing with writers such as Proust, Flaubert, Diderot. A chance encounter in the 1970s led her to the Chaos Theories of modern science, the concepts of which were already familiar to her because of her Proust studies. This in turn resulted in her 1996 book, *Chaos Theory, Complexity, Cinema and the Evolution of the French Novel*.

Bertrand Tavernier's films intrigued her the most of all those by current filmmakers as the expression of the principles of Proust's aesthetic as well as Chaos Theory. This book thus culminates a series of pursuits.

After twenty-four years of teaching at the University of Hawaii, she has moved to Santa Fe, New Mexico, the center for studies in Chaos and Complexity, to establish her own firm doing digital editing and educational videos.